Women in Snowboarding

This is the first book to examine the role of women in the origins, development and contemporary landscape of snowboarding. Focusing on organised and professional snowboarding, it explores the significance of women as participants, coaches, leaders and high-profile sport stars.

The book explores the history of snowboarding, the organisation of international snowboarding, issues related to facilities, competition formats that are the same for female and male riders, and injury risk, safeguarding, training and coaching. Before the concluding chapter, three elite snowboarders representing different epochs and riding styles – Åshild Lofthus, Stine Brun Kjeldaas and Kjersti Buaas – are introduced, whose narratives shed light on the main themes of the book. With a broad scope in terms of topics and academic disciplines, from medicine and biomechanics to the social sciences and sport governance, the book is grounded in sociology and gender studies.

This book is fascinating reading for scholars and students with an interest in the sociology of sport, coaching, sport management, sport history or interdisciplinary perspectives in sport science, or anybody with a passion for snowboarding.

Mari Kristin Sisjord is Professor of Sport Sociology in the Department of Sport and Social Sciences at the Norwegian School of Sport Sciences, Norway. Mari Kristin has published widely on issues related to youth sport, gender and sport, particularly with regard to women's experiences of coaching and sport leadership, and women and girls in snowboarding.

Women, Sport and Physical Activity

Edited by Elizabeth Pike, University of Hertfordshire, UK

The *Women, Sport and Physical Activity* series showcases work by leading international researchers and emerging scholars that offers new perspectives on the involvement of women in sport and physical activity. The series is interdisciplinary in scope, drawing on sociology, cultural studies, history, politics, gender studies, leisure studies, psychology, exercise science and coaching studies, and consists of two main strands: thematic volumes addressing key global issues in the study of women, sport and physical activity; and sport-specific volumes, each of which offers an overview of women's participation and leadership in a particular sport.
Available in this series:

Women in Judo
Edited by Mike Callan

Gender-Based Violence in Children's Sport
Gretchen Kerr

Gender Equality and the Olympic Programme
Michele K. Donnelly

The 2023 FIFA Women's World Cup
Politics, Representation, and Management
Edited by Adam Beissel, Verity Postlethwaite, Andrew Grainger and Julie E. Brice

Women in Snowboarding
Mari Kristin Sisjord

For more information about this series, please visit: https://www.routledge.com/Women-Sport-and-Physical-Activity/book-series/WSPA

Women in Snowboarding

Mari Kristin Sisjord

Routledge
Taylor & Francis Group

LONDON AND NEW YORK

First published 2023
by Routledge
4 Park Square, Milton Park, Abingdon, Oxon OX14 4RN

and by Routledge
605 Third Avenue, New York, NY 10158

Routledge is an imprint of the Taylor & Francis Group, an informa business

British Library Cataloguing-in-Publication Data
A catalogue record for this book is available from the British Library

Library of Congress Cataloging-in-Publication Data
Names: Sisjord, Mari Kristin, author.
Title: Women in snowboarding / Mari Kristin Sisjord.
Description: Abingdon, Oxon ; New York, NY : Routledge, 2024 |
Series: Women, sport and physical activity | Includes bibliographical references and index. |
Identifiers: LCCN 2023012461 | ISBN 9780367440152 (hardback) | ISBN 9781032557366 (paperback) | ISBN 9781003007098 (ebook)
Subjects: LCSH: Snowboarding—Social aspects. | Women snowboarders. | Women snowboarders—Biography.
Classification: LCC GV857.S57 S49 2024 | DDC 796.939082—dc23/eng/20230322
LC record available at https://lccn.loc.gov/2023012461

ISBN: 978-0-367-44015-2 (hbk)
ISBN: 978-1-032-55736-6 (pbk)
ISBN: 978-1-003-00709-8 (ebk)

DOI: 10.4324/9781003007098

Typeset in Times New Roman
by codeMantra

Contents

vi *Contents*

Series Editor Introduction

Elizabeth C.J. Pike

In recent years, the emergence of sports that present an alternative to traditional competitive activities has offered the potential to challenge the well-documented barriers to women's participation in sport. Scholars have variously described such sports as alternative, lifestyle, adventure, subcultural and postmodern activities. However, many of these sports have started to enter mainstream culture in order to gain the benefits of involvement in high-performance and commercially attractive events such as the Olympic Games. In so doing, the possibilities for subverting traditional gender norms and stereotypes are balanced against the need to be less countercultural in order to be acceptable in the mainstream.

This book addresses a relative lack of attention to gender issues in the sport of snowboarding. The author has considerable expertise in winter sports, with decades of scholarly activity related to snowboarding and gender. She presents new data from interviews with high-level experts in the snowboarding world to examine the position of women in the sport and the gendered power relations that they need to negotiate in order to be recognised as snowboarders.

Sisjord's book presents several unique perspectives: original data from women snowboarders who represent different historical periods in the development of the sport; the viewpoints of men working in the sport to consider how they may be social agents for change; and a multi-disciplinary analysis of the sport to illustrate the complexity of negotiating gender when participating in snowboarding as a woman.

In so doing, this book offers informative insights into the opportunities and challenges of developing sporting activities which might present a genuine alternative to traditional, male- and masculine-dominated sports culture. Mari Kristin Sisjord's contribution to the Routledge *Women, Sport and Physical Activity* series invites the reader to better understand how people engage in practices of gender and what this means for challenging gender inequality in order to ultimately achieve gender equity in and through sport.

1 Introduction

Over the last few decades, the pathways in which women used to enter into the world of sport have been examined extensively (e.g. Cahn, 2015; Hargreaves, 1994). History has shown that, over time, women gradually began to create their own ways in which they could carve a space for themselves in sports that were formerly only for the privilege of men. Since the 1970s and 1980s, we have witnessed a remarkable increase in the level of participation in sport among girls and women, particularly in wealthy post-industrial nations (Coakley & Pike, 2014) – something that applies to both organised sports and recreational sports. However, in general, female participants are still underrepresented in organised sports at every level, that is, from regular memberships to executive positions. It is also well documented that women make up a minority of roles in sport governance (Adriaanse, 2016; Elling et al., 2019) as well as in the field of coaching, especially when it comes to positions in elite-level coaching (Acosta & Carpenter, 2014; Fasting et al., 2017; Pfister, 2013).

The increase in women's participation in sport is particularly visible in activities that originally differed from or contrasted with traditional competitive sports (Thorpe & Olive, 2016). Snowboarding, along with other 'alternative sports' (Rinehart, 2000) – such as surfing, skating, rock climbing, kiting, BASE jumping, BMX cycling and the like – has in recent years evoked the interest of scholars, who in turn have come up with various new conceptualisations of such groups of sports, such as: 'lifestyle sports' (Wheaton, 2004), 'whiz sports' (Midol, 1993), 'action sports', 'risk sports', 'adventure sports', 'sub-culture sports' and 'postmodern sports' (Sisjord, 2014).

Of these activities, snowboarding in particular has always been a male-dominated sport. In terms of participation, studies indicate that girls and women compose about one-third (or less) of snowboarders, with a slight increase in recent years (Heino, 2000; Hunt, 2013; Sisjord, 2009, 2019a; Thorpe, 2005, 2007, 2011; Thorpe & Olive, 2016). The male/masculine domination has been an integral component to the development of the sport, as snowboarding styles and cultural expressions of the snowboarding culture are inherently linked to masculinity, what with these aspects being central

DOI: 10.4324/9781003007098-1

elements to its evolution, media representations, contests and competitions, and the organisation of the sport as a whole.

Since the emergence of snowboarding in the late 1960s and early 1970s, the sport has undergone major changes. From first being perceived as a product of counterculture – with its rebellious attitude – over time, snowboarding has entered into the mainstream and even developed into an Olympic sport. Indeed, during its relatively brief history, these major changes have occurred in various different areas of the sport. For example, the snowboarding culture is highly fragmented, with a plethora of snowboarding styles and participants, demonstrating varying levels of commitment and physical prowess (Thorpe, 2012). As Thorpe (2006) argues, to further understand the history, it is important that we contextualise snowboarding through its socio-political context, with specific reference to sociology and youth culture. By doing so, Thorpe identified two main periods of snowboarding culture, labelled as the pre-commercial and post-commercial eras, the latter of which occurred during the 1990s. Strittmatter et al. (2018), however, identified three main phases, but through the lens of a sport management/organisational perspective: first, the emergence of a cultural Industry and the significant roles of the early pioneers; second, the early commercialisation and professionalisation process; and third, the inclusion of snowboarding in the Olympic Games. Both perspectives on the development of the sport share similarities with respect to the first phase, but they diverge in the subsequent phases. Thorpe's focus is predominantly that of the commercial enterprise and mediation of the sport, whereas Strittmatter and her co-authors focus on the sportification of snowboarding, resulting in the development of snowboarding organisations and competitions.

The processes of the professionalisation and institutionalisation of snowboarding have further been described by several other scholars (Coates et al., 2010; Ojala, 2014; Rinehart, 2008; Spale, 2013; Steen-Johnsen, 2008). Yet, gender in snowboarding has attracted little attention in the research, meaning that we do not have sufficient knowledge of women's agency and inclusion in these processes. Ojala (2014), for example, focused on filming and photo shoots and the riders' roles and position in this activity. She did not mention gender prior to her conclusion, but she did still pose the question as to whether 'the regulative institutional element, from a sport management/organizational perspective, also [has] demolished some power relations between genders' (p. 121). She explained that women are rarely visible in snowboarding movies but seem to display a stronger status in competitions, which may be due to the organisers' interest in having more women involved. Thus, while gender has not been a sole focus in much of the research, even the little research that does touch upon the issue seems to indicate that there is evidence of the exclusion of women in major aspects of the sport, and that the inclusion of women may only be prioritised when it can be commercialised/monetised.

In general, gender issues – with particular reference to girls and women – have not had a prominent position in scholarly research on snowboarding, except for the few studies that solely focus on the topic, which will be further discussed throughout the book, particularly in Chapter 6. Gender issues are, at least, discussed by Holly Thorpe in her two books: *Snowboarding Bodies in Theory and Practice* (2011) and *Snowboarding: The Ultimate Guide* (2012). In her first book – the product of a seven-year project – she draws upon an extensive array of sources from six countries and discusses various aspects of the snowboarding culture in light of sociological theories, and from her own time as an experienced snowboarder. The second book is more practically oriented, as she provides an introduction to the sport and lifestyle of snowboarding, including techniques and equipment, an overview of key places and events, and a presentation of prominent snowboarding heroes, both women and men. The position of women and their agency in snowboarding culture is also explored by Susanna Howe, in her book *(Sick): A Cultural History of Snowboarding* (1998). Also, worth mentioning in this respect are two books written by professional snowboarders: *Pretty Good for a Girl: The Autobiography of a Snowboarding Pioneer* by Tina Basich and Kathleen Gasperini (2003) and *P3: Pipes, Parks, and Powder* by Todd Richards and Eric Blehm (2004). Both books provide rich insights into the ways in which young people got involved in snowboarding at a time when the sport was becoming more and more professionalised, especially with a gendered, masculine-dominated, youth culture as its backdrop.

In contrast to the authors mentioned above, I have not practiced snowboarding myself. However, I am well known within the skiing environment, having done downhill (and cross-country) skiing from my early childhood. My academic background brought me to the snowboarding back in 1996, as one of several activities I explored in a larger study about sport and youth culture. Some years later, in 2003, I was invited by the Norwegian Snowboard Federation (NSBF) to a workshop to give a speech on gender and sport, with particular focus on snowboarding. In the years to follow, I collaborated further with the NSBF on gender issues and continued my empirical research, which was later published, and which I will refer to in this book.

Following the overall objective of this book – analysing the position of women in snowboarding – my analysis will contain a broad scope in terms of the topics and academic disciplines explored, all of which is grounded in my own background of sociology, as well as the fields of medicine and biomechanics, as reflected in the section covering snowboarding injuries. The themes explored throughout the book are mainly related to organised, competitive snowboarding, although studies of recreational snowboarding are also included. In terms of introducing theoretical perspectives, I will refer to those being utilised in the publications I present and discuss. Consequently, a variety of viewpoints will be introduced, that is, conflicting opinions from other researchers and the interviewees, but the book will nonetheless be rooted in a basic understanding of gender as a social construct, embedded in power relations that impact the individual's social life and participation in various different fields. However, as the focus of the book is limited to women and snowboarding, I will not include LGBT perspectives. For the reader who is interested in exploring research on snowboarding, gender and sexuality, these themes are discussed in my 2019 text (Sisjord, 2019b).

The content of this book is based on existing research on snowboarding, supplemented by research from other relevant fields, such as coaching and sport governance. In addition to former research, supplementary information was needed in order to provide a more comprehensive picture of snowboarding in the present day – to achieve this, I conducted two studies, the first of which was a survey investigation and the second based on qualitative interviews with a total of eight participants involved in the sport, the result of which will be further elaborated on below.

Concerning snowboarding organisations, information from the web pages of the main international organisations – the World Snowboard Federation (WSF) and the International Ski Federation (FIS) – was used. Furthermore, a survey investigation was sent to the national snowboard federations listed as members of the WSF and/or FIS, which will be described in Chapter 3. To supplement this, I also conducted an interview with the president of the WSF, Satu Järvelä.

For this book, I also interviewed four snowboarding coaches: three men and one woman, all of whom are from Norway, for convenience given the Norwegian context this book was written in. The coaches include: two male coaches who work for the national snowboarding teams, that of the senior and recruit teams, respectively. The third male coach works at a secondary school where the students are offered a combination of snowboarding practice and a regular secondary education, carried out over three years (students in the age group of 16–19 years). The female interviewee is a former coach for the same secondary school. When the interview took place, she was working as a coach for a mixed-gender group of younger snowboarders at a local snowboarding club.

In addition to the above interviews, I have included interviews with three former elite-level snowboarders, all Norwegian women, who represent different periods of the development of snowboarding as well as different disciplines and riding styles. These interviews are discussed separately in Chapter 7, although their interviews are also referred to in two other chapters covering the topics of snowboarding disciplines, facilities and injuries in Chapter 4, and training and coaching in Chapter 5. The former elite snowboarders are Åshild Lofthus, Stine Brun Kjeldaas and Kjersti Buaas.

In terms of methodology, all eight interviews were tape-recorded and transcribed verbatim. The interview with the WSF president was held in English, and the rest in Norwegian. In cases of quotations presented in the text, these were translated into English, first by myself with the Norwegian quote in parenthesis, and then corrected by the professional language consultant I used for the whole book. In regard to ethical considerations, the study proposal was guided by the Data Protection Official for Research, who evaluates proposals from scholars of Norwegian universities, university colleges, hospitals and research institutes. The proposal covers a plan for data collection including interview guide(s) and a description of the sample. The interviewees were informed about the voluntary nature of participation and their right to withdraw without providing any explanation. The interviewees were given a draft of the chapters they were cited in, alongside the Norwegian version in cases where I provided a quotation. I received a small number of minor comments, which I have taken into consideration.

With respect to identity of the interviewees, anonymity was out of question for the president of the WSF and the named elite-level snowboarders, for obvious reasons. The coaches, however, are referred to solely by their job title, given that this seemed to be the most relevant way to describe and highlight their experiences and perspectives of the issues discussed. Admittedly, the snowboarding milieu in Norway is so small that the interviewees may easily be traced – something that the interviewees were well aware of when they consented to the interview and when reading the drafts of the book.

The book is organised into the following chapters:

1 Introduction
2 The history of snowboarding: from counterculture to the Olympic Games
3 Structure and gender inequality in snowboarding organisations
4 Snowboarding disciplines, facilities and injuries
5 Training and coaching in snowboarding
6 Female snowboarders in various contexts
7 Female elite snowboarders representing different epochs and snowboarding styles
8 Concluding remarks

References

Acosta, V. & Carpenter, L.J. (2014). *Women in Intercollegiate Sport. A Longitudinal National Study Thirty-Seven Year Update, 1977–2014.* Brooklyn College. DOI:10.1123/wspaj.9.2.141

Adriaanse, J.A. (2016). Gender diversity in the governance of sport associations: The Sydney scoreboard global index of participation. *Journal of Business Ethics, 137*(1), 149–160. DOI:10.1007/s10551-015-2550-3

Basich, T. & Gasperini, K. (2003). *Pretty Good for a Girl: The Autobiography of a Snowboarder Pioneer.* HarperCollins.

Cahn, S.K. (2015). *Coming on Strong. Gender and Sexuality in Women's Sport* (2nd ed.). University of Illinois Press.

Coakley, J.J. & Pike, E. (2014). *Sports in Society: Issues and Controversies* (2nd ed.). McGraw-Hill.

Coates, E., Clayton, B., & Humberstone, B. (2010). A battle for control: Exchanges of power in the subculture of snowboarding. *Sport in Society, 13*(7/8), 1082–1101. DOI:10.1080/17430431003779999

Elling, A., Hovden, J. & Knoppers, A. (2019). *Gender Diversity in European Sport Governance*. Routledge, Taylor & Francis.

Fasting, K., Sisjord, M.K. & Sand, T.S. (2017). Norwegian elite-level coaches: Who are they? *Scandinavian Sports Studies Forum 8*, 29–47.

Hargreaves, J. (1994). *Sporting Females: Critical Issues in the History and Sociology of Women's Sport*. Routledge.

Heino, R. (2000). New sports: What is so punk about snowboarding? *Journal of Sport and Social Issues, 24*(2), 176–191.

Howe, S. (1998). *(Sick) a Cultural History of Snowboarding*. St Martin's Press.

Hunt, K.A. (2013). A business case analysis of the snowboarding industry. *Journal of Business Case Studies, 9*(2), 111–120. http://www.cluteinstitute.com

Midol, N. (1993). Cultural dissents and technical innovations in the 'whiz' sports. *International Review for the Sociology of Sport, 28*(1), 23–29. DOI:10.1177/101269029302800102

Ojala, A.-L. (2014). Institutionalization in professional freestyle snowboarding – Finnish professional riders' perceptions. *European Journal for Sport and Society, 11*(2), 103–126. DOI:10.1080/16138171.2014.11687936

Pfister, G. (2013). Outsiders: Female coaches intruding upon a male domain. In Pfister, G. & Sisjord, M.K. (Eds.), *Gender and Sport. Changes and Challenges* (pp. 71–99). Waxmann.

Richards, T. & Blehm, E. (2004). *P3: Pipes, Parks, and Powder*. Regan Books.

Rinehart, R.E. (2000). Arriving sports: Alternative to formal sports. In Coakley, J. & Dunning, E. (Eds.), *Handbook of Sports Studies* (pp. 504–521). Sage Publications.

Rinehart, R.E. (2008). Exploiting a new generation: Corporate Branding and the Co-Optation of Action Sport. In Giardina, M.D. & Donnelly, K.M. (Eds.), *Youth Culture and Sport. Identity, Power, and Politics* (pp.71–89). Routledge.

Sisjord, M.K. (2009). Fast-girls, babes and the invisible girls. Gender relations in snowboarding. *Sport in Society, 12*(10), 1299–1316. DOI:10.1080/17430430903204801

Sisjord, M.K. (2014). Assessing the sociology of sport: On lifestyle sport and gender. *International Review for the Sociology of Sport, 50*(4–5), 596–600. DOI: 1080/17430430903204801.

Sisjord, M. K. (2019a). Snowboarding: Women's agency from outsiders to insiders in the organisation. In Elling, A., Hovden, J. & A. Knoppers, A. (Eds.), *Gender Diversity in European Sport Governance* (pp. 165–175). Routledge, Taylor & Francis.

Sisjord, M.K. (2019b). Gender, sexuality, and sports: Shifting attitudes in snowboarding culture. In Maguire, J., Falcous, M. & Liston, K. (Eds.), *The Business and Culture of Sports: Society, Politics, Economy, Environment* (Vol. 1, pp. 321–335). Macmillan Publishers Ltd. ISBN 978-0-02-866498-9. S 321-335.

Spale, C. (2013). *Netzwerkstrukturen im Szenesport und die Bedeutung kommerzieller Akteure. Eine Analyse am Beispiel des Snowboardsports*. [Network structures in scene sports and the significance of commercial actors. An analysis based on the example from the sport of snowboarding]. Dissertation, Bern: University of Bern, Department for Sports Science.

Steen-Johnsen, K. (2008). Networks and the organization of identity: The case of Norwegian snowboarding. *European Sport Management Quarterly, 8*(4), 337–358. DOI:10.1080/16184740802461629

Strittmatter, A.M., Kilvinger, B., Bodemar, A., Skille, E.Å. & Kurscheidt, M. (2018). Dual governance structures in action sports: Institutionalization processes of professional snowboarding. *Sport in Society, 22*(10), 1655–1673. DOI:10.1080/17430437.2018.1440696

Thorpe, H. (2005). Jibbing the gender order: Females in the Snowboarding Culture. *Sport in Society, 8*(1), 76–100. DOI:10.1080/1743043052000316632

Thorpe, H. (2006). Beyond "decorative sociology": Contextualizing female surf, skate, and snow boarding. *Sociology of Sport Journal, 23*(3), 205–228.

Thorpe, H. (2007). Snowboarding. In Thorpe, H. & Booth, D. (Eds.), *Berkshire Encyclopedia of Extreme Sports* (pp. 286–294). Berkshire Publishing.

Thorpe, H. (2011). *Snowboarding Bodies in Theory and Practice*. Palgrave Macmillan.

Thorpe, H. (2012). *Snowboarding: The Ultimate Guide*. Greenwood Press.

Thorpe, H. & Olive, R. (2016). *Women in Action Sport Cultures: Identity, Politics and Experience*. Palgrave Macmillan.

Wheaton, B. (2004). Introduction: Mapping the lifestyle sport-scape. In Wheaton, B. (Ed.), *Understanding Lifestyle Sports* (pp. 1–28). Routledge.

2 The history of snowboarding

From counterculture to the Olympic Games

This chapter provides a short overview of the historical development of snowboarding. In line with the phases suggested by Thorpe (2006) and Strittmatter et al. (2018), I start with the first period – that of the emergence of the sport through youth culture and counterculture. Following on from that, I will briefly elaborate on the expansion of the snowboarding industry and its early contests. Thereafter, I will describe the organisation of snowboarding, leading into its sportification and inclusion of the Olympic Games.

Counterculture and the new leisure movement

Snowboarding emerged in the late 1960s and 1970s in North America. The early pioneers embodied the idealism of youth culture and counterculture, embracing snowboarding as a free, cooperative, enjoyable and individualistic activity. Indeed, as part of the new leisure movement, snowboarders subscribed to anti-establishment counterculture values and a do-it-yourself philosophy (Thorpe, 2007). Adherents to this philosophy were reacting against the overarching conformity and stifling nature of society; counterculture inspired individuals to see themselves as original works of art and to be true to one's self (Humphrey, 2003). The movement thus also expressed social dissatisfaction in the realm of sport and the adherents of these new types of sports, like snowboarding, did not conform to the prevailing definitions of conventional sport (Humphrey, 1996). The new leisure movement's philosophy emphasised non-competition, cooperation and self-expression, characterised by experimenting with activities that require motor skills, creativity or risk-taking, but with an emphasis on fun and personal growth (Donnelly, 1988). Furthermore, a significant feature of these sports was grassroots participation and a commitment to collective expressions, attitudes and social identities that developed in and around the activity (Wheaton, 2004).

In the 1970s and 1980s, the punk movement further influenced the artistic sensibility of the new leisure movement. Punks emphasised personal honesty and integrity and retained the countercultural critique of late capitalism, mass communication, and mass consumption. Their politics and philosophies were

DOI: 10.4324/9781003007098-2

best explored and articulated through the tenets of art (Humphrey, 2003). The influence of punk and skateboarding had a major impact on the development of snowboarding in the early 1990s with its increasingly urban, aggressive attitude and clothing style, which was also inspired by hip-hop imagery (Howe, 1998). Snowboarders embodied the masculine images of the skateboarders in oversized, baggy clothing, commonly wearing flannels (Anderson, 1999; Howe, 1998) which contributed to the marginalisation of female participation. Style is an important aspect in snowboarding as it is not just manifested in the choice of clothing, but in the equipment and language, allowing people to distinguish between insiders and outsiders – a common theme in the early research of snowboarding culture (e.g. Anderson, 1999; Heino, 2000).

Research of this early phase was much inspired by youth culture studies, particularly studies on the counterculture or subculture tradition conducted by the Centre for Contemporary Cultural Studies in Birmingham. These studies examined spectacular, resistive youth groups focusing on specific activities, values and subcultural styles (music, hairstyle, language) that distinguished certain groups of youths from the wider culture (Brake, 1985; Hall & Jefferson, 1975; Hebdidge, 1979).

Development of the snowboarding industry and early contests

The development of snowboarding is intrinsically connected to the development of the snowboarding industry in the United States. The *Snurfer* is usually considered to have been a breakthrough for snowboarding, as it was the first commercially available snowboard-like piece of equipment (Gutman & Frederick, 2004). It was created in the mid-1960s in Michigan by Sherman Poppen as a toy for his daughters, which in itself is an interesting observation in terms of gender dynamics in snowboarding. The *Snurfer* was put into production, and as it gained popularity through the 1970s, others became interested in the industry, and snowboarding expanded. Among the first to produce snowboards were the American surfer Dimitrije Milovich, inspired by his friend Wayne Stoveken – another trailblazer in the surfing and snowboarding industry. Milovich set up the company Winterstick Snowboard company in Utah in 1975 and began selling the first technologically advanced boards, shaped like a mini surfboard, even including a 'control skeg' (Humphrey, 1996, p. 6). Later, Jake Burton (with a background in alpine skiing) and Tom Sims (a former top professional skater) gravitated towards the board industry, and influenced the development of riding styles (Howe, 1998; Humphrey, 1996).

The pioneers and early snowboarding companies went on to establish their own competitions – starting in the early 1980s – which were rooted in the snowboarding communities themselves, thus helping the sport retain its philosophy while contributing to its commercialisation of snowboarding (Humphrey, 1997). In essence, the snowboarding pioneers were almost all men, but it is important to note that a few professional female snowboarders also contributed to the development and commercialisation of the sport through the late 1980s and early 1990s, including Tina Basich, Shannon Dunn and Michele Taggart (Howe, 1998; Thorpe, 2005, 2011).

The first national and international snowboarding competitions were held in the early 1980s (Batuev et al., 2020). Obviously, with men as the standard. For example, in the first half-pipe competitions, there was no separate women's division; the few women who did participate, competed in the same events as the men. The situation remained as such until the late 1980s, when a separate division was established for female riders across each of the sport's various disciplines (Gutman & Frederick, 2004). In 1988, the first half-pipe competition to be held in Stratton, Vermont, had both a male and a female division. Separate women's categories encouraged female participants, and in contrast to other board sports, female inclusion was highly valued. The first Winter X Games held in 1997 included male and female categories in slopestyle and boardercross events and has continued to provide an arena for both women and men to showcase their snowboarding skills. The opportunities for women's participation continued into the 1998 Olympic Games in Nagano, where snowboarding was the only snow sport that did not differentiate between female and male athletes. In the half-pipe competition, they performed on the same courses and were judged based on the same criteria as the male riders (Thorpe, 2005).

For many years, however, female snowboarders were not taken seriously in the marketplace or in the media. In fact, prior to the mid-1990s, there were no gender-specific boards or equipment sold on the market, and given that men are the default in this sport, that meant that female snowboarders had to wear clothing and use equipment made for men. When it comes to the boards, there are technical reasons as to why women should have different snowboards, namely because women are typically lighter, have a narrower stance, and have smaller feet (Thorpe, 2005). The professional snowboarders Tina Basich and Shannon Dunn played important roles in this regard. Their sponsors recognised their marketing value and in 1994 they were 'the first girls to release signature pro model snowboards' (Basich & Gasperini, 2003, p. 102). The two worked with different snowboarding companies, with Dunn represented by Sims and Basich represented by Kemper. It turned out to be a success, and from 1995 numerous companies started producing female-specific boards with graphics chosen and designed by women (Thorpe, 2005).

In regard to their clothing, the baggy style was manufactured with male riders in mind, which many girls and women found uncomfortable – both physically when wearing them, and because of the masculine image the clothes conveyed. Among the participants in Anderson's study (1999), the few female interviewees explained that they preferred warmer clothing (not flannels) but admitted to adhering to the snowboarding style and culture. Likewise, as revealed in my first study of snowboarding conducted in 1996, female snowboarders preferred clothes from second-hand stores instead of the baggy style of the male riders. In doing so, they avoided the uncomfortable oversized clothes, and instead developed their own style that fit well with their personal image and the alternative youth culture that had attracted them to the sport (Sisjord, 2005).

Tina Basich describes the problems she faced while wearing men's snowboarding outfits because she had no other choice: She had to roll up the sleeves of her tops and fold up the trouser legs and wear a belt just to hold them up (Basich & Gasperini, 2003). She noted that the oversized outfit 'was only cool to a point. We were pro riders and needed clothing that fit, and the monster clothing was getting in the way' (p. 102). Once more girls and women started snowboarding, a growing demand for women-specific equipment emerged. At that point, Basich and her pro-snowboarding friend, Shannon Dunn approached Swag snowboard clothing, which led to an opportunity for them to launch a women's clothing line, which they called Pron – all produced in pastel colours. Soon after, other companies saw the potential in women's clothing, in terms of different styles and colours, and the industry expanded (Howe, 1998).

The organisation of snowboarding

Although snowboarding is perceived as an offshoot of surfing and skateboarding (Howe, 1998; Humphrey, 1996; Young, 2004), its relation to skiing should also be noted, as the participants use the same resorts (Edensor & Richards, 2007). The history of snowboarding reveals numerous conflicts between skiers and snowboarders on the slopes, and between ski resort owners and snowboarders, resorts in which snowboarders were previously excluded from the slopes (Heino, 2000). The contrast between the different origins, cultures and backgrounds of skiing on the one hand, and the snowboarding on the other, manifested in disagreements between the International Snowboard Federation (ISF) and the FIS, as well as in the riders' attitudes and behaviours when it came to competitions and contests. The ISF was established in 1990 by riders and for riders, with the aim of bringing the world's best snowboarders together to test their skills in an environment that embraced competitiveness, while still maintaining the importance of having fun.

The IFS set the standards for snowboarding competitions which contributed to the development of the sport becoming an Olympic discipline in 1998 (Rails, 2011). To the dismay of IFS supporters though, the International Olympic Committee (IOC) recognised FIS as the sport's official governing body instead (Humphrey, 2003), which provoked resistance among the 'core' snowboarders. Terje Haakonsen was widely regarded as a 'snowboard legend' after refusing to participate in the Olympic Games in Nagano in 1998 – when snowboarding was introduced into the institution – thus distancing himself and snowboarding from the Olympic movement with the expression:

'Snowboarding is everything the Olympics isn't' (Lidz, 1997, p. 114). Heino (2000) verbalised this opposition to the Olympics as basically 'a resistance to the discipline of bureaucracy and power' (p. 189). Howe (1998) explains the poor reputation the FIS has among snowboarders due to it 'being militaristic and closed minded' (p. 154), whereas the IFS was known to have the snowboarders' best interests at heart. The contradictions between IFS [replaced by the World Snowboarding Federation (WSF) in 2002] and the FIS have influenced the organisational development of snowboarding. It has also influenced which different contests (FIS vs WSF arrangements) snowboarders choose to recognise (Burton, 2003; Humphrey, 2003). More changes have, however, cropped up over the last few years, which will be discussed in the next chapter.

References

Anderson, K. (1999). Snowboarding. The construction of gender in an emerging sport. *Journal of Sport and Social Issues, 23*(1), 55–79.

Basich, T. & Gasperini, K. (2003). *Pretty Good for a Girl: The Autobiography of a Snowboarder Pioneer.* Harper Collins.

Batuev, M., Zipp, S. & Robinson, L. (2020). Snowboarding and skateboarding. In Nauright, J. & Zipp, S. (Eds.), *Routledge Handbook of Global Sport* (pp. 446–463). Routledge.

Brake, M. (1985). *Comparative Youth Culture. The Sociology of Youth Cultures and Youth Subcultures in America, Britain and Canada.* Routledge and Kegan Paul.

Burton, J. (2003). The essence is fun. In Rinehart, R.E. & Sydnor, S. (Eds.), *To the Extreme. Alternative Sports, Inside and Out* (pp. 401–406). State University of New York Press.

Donnelly, P. (1988). Sport as a site for 'popular' resistance. In Gruneau, R. (Ed.), *Popular Cultures and Political Practices* (pp. 69–82). Garamond Press.

Edensor, T. & Richards, S. (2007). Snowboarders vs skiers: Contested choreographies of the slopes. *Leisure Studies, 26*(1), 97–114. DOI:10.1080/02614360500372224

Gutman, B. & Frederick, S. (2004). *Catching Air: The Excitement and Daring of Individual Action Sports –Snowboarding, Skateboarding, BMX Biking, In-Line Skating.* Citadel Press.

Hall, S. & Jefferson, T. (1975). *Resistance Through Rituals. Youth Cultures in Post-War Britain.* Hutchinson.

Hebdidge, D. (1979). *Subculture. The Meaning of Style.* Routledge.

Heino, R. (2000). New sports: What is so punk about snowboarding? *Journal of Sport and Social Issues, 24*(2), 176–191.

Howe, S. (1998). *(Sick) a Cultural History of Snowboarding.* St Martin's Press.

Humphrey, D. (1996). Snowboarders: Bodies out of control and conflict. Sporting traditions. *Journal of the Australian Society for Sports History, 13*(1), 3–23.

Humphrey, D. (1997). 'Shredheads go mainstream'? Snowboarding and alternative youth. *International Review for the Sociology of Sport, 32*(2), 147–160. DOI:10.1177/101269097032002003

Humphrey, D. (2003). Selling out snowboarding. In Rinehart, R.E. & Sydnor, S. (Eds.), *To the Extreme. Alternative Sports, Inside and Out* (pp. 407–428). State University of New York Press.

Lidz, F. (1997). Lord of the board. *Sports Illustrated, 87*(25), 114–119.

Rails. (2011). *Project Rails: Reviewing and Analyzing the International Level of Snowboarding*. Master Dissertation. University of Oslo.

Sisjord, M.K. (2005). Snowboard – en kjønnet ungdomskultur. [Snowboarding – a gendered youth culture]. *Tidsskrift for ungdomsforskning* [*Journal of Youth Research*], *5*(2), 65–82.

Strittmatter, A.M., Kilvinger, B., Bodemar, A., Skille, E.Å. & Kurscheidt, M. (2018). Dual governance structures in action sports: Institutionalization processes of professional snowboarding. *Sport in Society, 22*(10), 1655–1673. DOI:10.1080/17430437 .2018.1440696

Thorpe, H. (2005). Jibbing the gender order: Females in the snowboarding culture. *Sport in Society, 8*(1), 76–100. DOI:10.1080/1743043052000316632

Thorpe, H. (2006). Beyond 'decorative sociology': Contextualizing female surf, skate, and snow boarding. *Sociology of Sport Journal, 23*(3), 205–228.

Thorpe, H. (2007). Snowboarding. In Thorpe, H. & Booth, D. (Eds.), *Berkshire Encyclopedia of Extreme Sports* (pp. 286–294). Berkshire Publishing.

Thorpe, H. (2011). *Snowboarding Bodies in Theory and Practice*. Palgrave Macmillan.

Wheaton, B. (2004). Introduction: Mapping the lifestyle sport-scape. In Wheaton, B. (Ed.), *Understanding Lifestyle Sports* (pp. 1–28). Routledge.

Young, A. (2004). Being the 'alternative' in an alternative subculture: Gender differences in the experience of young women and men in skateboarding and snowboarding. *Avante, 10*(3), 69–81.

3   Structure and gender inequality in snowboarding organisations

The way in which the sport of snowboarding is officially organised and struc-
tured came about as a result of an increase in the number of snowboarding
contests being held, and thus the need for more governance. Over the years,
many different actors and interests have been involved, from the commercial
industry of the X Games and Dew Tour, to the non-profit organisation World
Snowboard Federation (WSF), and the more traditional sporting institution,
represented by the International Ski Federation (FIS). The history and way
that this sport has organised itself on a structural level has been characterised
by tensions between the WSF and the FIS, originating from a disagreement
about the nature of snowboarding's governing body for the Olympic Games
and about qualification contests for the games (Rails, 2011). In later years, the
WSF and FIS apparently reached an agreement about how international snowboarding should be organised, and entered into mutual collaboration through
the World Snowboarding Point List (WSPL), a ranking that incorporates the
results of competitions held by both FIS and WSF. In regard to the FIS's
benefits of collaborating on WSPL, this is evident in their access to WSF's
rich collection dedicated to the digital history of snowboarding and WSF's
authority in the development of amateur snowboarding through its grassroots
programmes, events and other activities. Whereas the WSF has acknowledged
that snowboarding will benefit from FIS's involvement due to their status as
the sole, representative governing body, providing athletes with a clear international pathway into the Olympics. Both organisations have agreed to continue with this partnership, in which the breadth of knowledge and opinions
can be brought together and unified in their joint aim of elevating the sport.
(http://www.worldsnowboarding.org/about-wst/)

Given the fact that the WSF and FIS are the main organisations at the
head of international snowboarding today, I will concentrate on these in the
following discussion. First, I will start by providing a short description of
each organisation, and thereafter outline the extent and nature of their gender-
based policies and gender representation. I will then present a survey investigation so as to provide more detailed information about the reality of gender
equality and such policies across a number of different national snowboarding

DOI: 10.4324/9781003007098-3

organisations. The chapter will end with a discussion on the implications of gender-biased representation within these kinds of organisations.

The World Snowboard Federation

The WSF was established in 2002 as the successor of the International Snowboard Federation (ISF). The WSF is a non-profit organisation that exclusively works towards the development of snowboarding as a sport on all levels, including: competitive snowboarding, education, adaptive snowboarding and the organisation of activities for riders of any age. The WSF represents a network of national snowboarding associations that cooperate worldwide, all with the common goal of advancing the sport. The overarching organisation founded several snowboarding competitions, such as: World Rookie Tour for athletes under 18, the WSF Banked Slalom Tours and WSF Pro Woman. Until recently, Ticket To Ride (TTR) – the World Tour for snowboarders – was organised in collaboration with the WSF. The WSF also organises educational programmes and workshops for instructors, competition judges, technical delegates and club managers.

(https://www.worldsnowboardfederation.org/about-world-snowboard-federation)

The International Ski Federation

The FIS is the governing body responsible for the organisation of snowboarding as a sport, along with other ski sports such as alpine skiing, cross-country skiing and ski jumping. The FIS includes a snowboarding committee with representatives from several nations. In many of its member nations, snowboarding is organised as part of the national ski federation, meaning that their snowboarding representatives have a voice in the FIS system. The FIS organises their own World Cup, and as the organisation is also responsible for snowboarding in the Olympics, they therefore oversee the Olympic qualification competitions too (Rails, 2011).

Gender policy in the WSF and FIS

According to the WSF statutes, the topic of gender is covered by Article 5 – Neutrality:

> The WSF is neutral. The WSF rejects all forms and means of discrimination against individuals, groups of people, organisations, National Snowboard Associations or countries on grounds of politics, ethnic origin, gender, language, religion and on any other grounds. The WSF promotes and supports with all means gender equality in its activities.
> (https://www.worldsnowboardfederation.org/wsf/corporate-documents/)

Other than the mention of gender in Article 5, there WSF has no specific gender policy. The lack of a mandate focusing on gender distribution is reflected in the composition of its executive board (by 2020, the last updated web page): The WSF is run by one female president, four male vice presidents, one male deputy chief, and four out of five of the other board members are men. Furthermore, the WSF has elected representatives: three male event representatives, and three riders' representatives, of whom one is male and the other two female. The secretary general is also a woman. In other words, four out of 17 board members are women. It is worth noting though that, while the president of the WSF is a woman (for the period 2018–2022), this is far from common in sport organisations.

(https://www.worldsnowboardfederation.org/wsf/executive-board/)

The gender bias is also reflected in the WSF membership list. Among the 48 associations registered as members in 2018, women counted for about 20% of the contact persons listed (Sisjord, 2019). In order to promote the participation of women in the sport, the WSF established WSF Pro Women in 2015, with the event series described on the homepage as:

A dedicated umbrella initiative, serving women snowboarding events. Launched by the World Snowboard Federation in 2015, WSF Pro Women seeks to highlight a girls and women friendly approach to snowboarding that resonates through community-based activities, and ensuring shared experiences on the snow is an integral part of all WSF Pro Women events.
(https://www.world snowboardfederation.org/wsf-pro-women/)

The focus of WSF Pro Women seems to mainly be that of events, with its core objective being to increase female participation and skill enhancement through cooperation with high-profile ambassadors from different countries, who are listed on the website. The information available about WSF Pro Women only relates to activities for the season 2016–2017, with no other, recent information having been announced since. Looking at the WSF homepage, it would seem that it may potentially have been replaced by the Girls Shred Sessions initiative.

The Girls Shred Sessions are arranged by QParks – one of the major snow park designers and builders. They organise contests and tours for snowboarders and free-skiers in parks located in Italy, Austria, Germany and Switzerland. The intention for the Girls Shred Sessions is to encourage women to visit their parks and to help them develop their snowboarding skills with the assistance of experienced coaches – all for free. During these sessions, the riders are invited to develop 'shred skills' in a relaxed and easy-going atmosphere and to socialise with other, motivated female snowboarders. The project started in 2012, but it was only mentioned for the first time on the WSF website in 2018.

(https://www.worldsnowboardfederation.org/2017/12/20/girls-shred-sessions-2018-info-schedule/)

The concept behind Girls Shred Sessions looks like it was developed and implemented in Austria, as the most recent invitation to the activities is written in German, and the destinations and resorts are all in Austria. The target group, however, seems to be broader than just that of the members who attend the WSF ProWomen events, and seeing as it's QParks that organise these sessions, another intention here, besides facilitating the skills development of female snowboarders, may be to attract more customers to their snow parks and resorts.

(https://www.girlsshredsessions.com//page/info/)

In an interview with WSF President Satu Järvelä, she explained that there had been a change in focus on gender issues within the association since Pro Women was established. Their policy is now more widely directed towards the all groups of female snowboarders and towards working alongside national associations in order to encourage them to promote women's snowboarding in their own countries, for example by hosting women-only events and camps. In that regard, she emphasised that there are still great differences in the state of women's snowboarding in different countries, with the Nordic countries and Canada, for example, proving to be much further ahead in their efforts than others.

The FIS is also heavily male dominated: one male president and four vice presidents. The secretary general is also a man. Among the other 12 council members, there are four women. Additionally, there are also two athletes' commission representatives: one of each sex.

(https://www.fis-ski.com/en/inside-fis/organisation/fis-council/dean-gosper)

FIS also consists of several committees dedicated to the governance of various different disciplines, in which snowboarding is represented by the freestyle skiing and free-skiing committee. The head of this committee is a man, and the vice-chairs for snowboarding and for freestyle/snowboarding are both men, whereas vice-chair for freestyle is a woman. The five members of the snowboard committee are all males, while the freestyle/snowboard committee consists of one woman and two men.

(https://www.fis-ski.com/DB/general/committees.html?parentid=176&committeeid=100198&nationcode=)

FISs homepage provides no information about any specific gender policy or initiatives dedicated promoting women's snowboarding. It should, however, be noted that FIS had a participant on a pathway arranged with the purpose at empowering female coaches. The course is part of a programme called WISH – the Women in Sport High-performance pathway – which is one element of the International Olympic Committee (IOC)'s action plan aimed at meeting gender-equality commitments and objectives.

(https://olympics.com/ioc/news/empowering-female-coaches-a-week-in-the-life-of-the-wish-programme)

The representative from FIS (ski/snowboarding) was from snowboarding (Elizabeth Pike, personal communication).

It seems reasonable then that any projects with this focus are instead initiated by the individual national federations, as will be discussed in the next section based on the survey investigation as mentioned in Chapter 1.

The survey investigation

The survey investigation was conducted via an online questionnaire, available to participants between February and June 2020, organised and initiated by research assistant Olav Skrudland at our university (The Norwegian School of Sport Sciences). The online questionnaire was addressed and sent to potential participants via email. The email contained information about the survey, including: the purpose of the study, the name of the responsible researcher (Mari Kristin Sisjord), their email address, ethical considerations and a link to the questionnaire. A reminder was sent out a few weeks after emailing the organisations, and another was issued a month later. The last respondent registered to participate on 15 June.

The sample unit was defined as being a member association of WSF and/ or FIS. The sample was composed according to the following procedure: first, we visited the WSF and FIS homepages to identify the member organisations, and then noted/searched for email addresses to the organisations (or contact persons of the organisations). A few were not possible to trace, and some appeared to be a member of both WSF and FIS. The sample then resulted in $n = 136$. Among the 65 people who opened the link to the questionnaire, 48 responded, and of those, 20 did not answer all the questions. We addressed the wording: Which federation/association do you represent? And nationality of the federation/association? The terms 'association' and 'federation' are most commonly used by the various organisations, and some were registered in the organisation's national language.

In regard to the response rate, we received no emails in return (meaning emails that didn't reach the intended recipient) and cannot therefore explain why only half of the original sample opened the link to the questionnaire. The headline of the email was *Women in snowboarding – research project Norwegian School of Sport Sciences*. The email further informed the recipients that the survey concerned organisational matters, such as the composition of the boards, national teams, participation in contests and so on in their country, with particular focus on gender distribution. Whether the topic appeared irrelevant, out of interest, or controversial, is hard to say. However, one potential explanation could be that the members of the organisations we contacted were possibly overloaded with similar requests or had limited capacity to take on any extra tasks. Likewise, we cannot explain the opened links that did not receive response. Taking into account that online surveys commonly receive low response rates, however, we can presume that the results we did receive are representative enough to provide a certain indication of the present situation.

Due to the fact that we received incomplete questionnaires from several members of the organisations contacted, the total number (*n*) recorded below will vary depending on the question (variables). It should also be noted that several of the respondents did not reveal the name of the organisation they were a member of and responding on behalf of. For those who did report which organisation they were affiliated with, 27 answered FIS, 11 answered WSF, and 8 answered 'others' which were supplemented with the name of said organisation. In respect to the type of organisation they were a member of, 8 answered 'independent snowboard federation', 22 answered 'multisport federation' and 2 answered 'other organised form'. For those that listed the multisport federation option, the majority mentioned skiing disciplines, associated with the FIS.

In the following section, I will present the data relating to the gender composition of the executive boards and national teams, and whether the organisation in question has a gender policy. The gender distribution of the executive boards is shown in Table 3.1.

Table 3.1 reflects the domination of men on the national organisations' executive boards. In total, women make up about 20% of these roles (60 out of 307). Except for the two women representing riders/athletes, men outnumber women in every position. Overall, the gender bias within these national associations, skewed in favour of men, is most obvious in the roles perceived to be most powerful, such as that of president and vice-president, which thus reflects the situation facing gender equality as a whole within WSF as well as the FIS.

The results resonate with existing research on women's representation in sport governance. For example, an audit of the gender ratio on the boards of 45 national sport organisations collected through the Sydney Scoreboard (an interactive website that tracks women's presence on sport boards

Table 3.1 Gender distribution in different board positions

Board position	Female	Male	Total
President	3	22	25
Vice-President(s)	6	26	32
Board members[a]	39	185	224
Event representative[b]	1	3	4
Rider/athlete representatives[a]	2	0	2
Others[c]	9	11	20
Total	60	247	307

[a]Only includes those who responded with exact numbers of female vs. male members. Some answered that they have both but did not specify the amount.
[b]Only one organisation.
[c]Examples: Head of snowboarding department, female responsible, member executive committee, snowboard and free-ski coordinator, facility manager, technical adviser, alpine and snowboard specialist, and secretary general.

internationally), showed that women's representation in roles such as board directors, board chairs, and chief executives varied between 10 and 20% (Adriaanse, 2016). Based on a study of 11 European countries, the results reveal significant variations in female representation on national boards, ranging from about 10% to 40%, with Norway and Sweden having the highest level of female representation (Elling et al., 2019). The study showed slow progress in several countries and that an increase in women's representation is a political issue that requires attention and specific initiatives to achieve.

In regard to the composition of each country's national teams in snowboarding, 23 out of 31 respondents answered this question: 18 answered that their country had gender-mixed teams, 2 answered that men and women were split into different teams and 3 answered that they only had men's teams. None responded that they only had a women's team. The gender distribution on the teams can be seen in Table 3.2.

The results above show that gender-mixed teams are mostly common, for which women make up a little over one-third of the total number. However, when looking at all of the columns together, the proportion of female athletes participating at the national level decreases. We also included a question regarding – which competitions the female and male athletes usually participate in and which resulted in a long list of various competitions. The most common were the World Cup, European Cup, Olympic Games, X Games, Dew Tour, Burton US Open and other national championships. In general, the results do not distinguish much between women and men.

We also asked whether the athletes received financial support from the federation (i.e. salary, sponsorship), to which 13 answered 'yes' and 12 answered 'no'. None of the respondents mentioned gender differences in regard to which athletes received the financial support. The respondents were additionally asked whether they had any idea about differences between women and men in regard to private sponsorship. For this question, 18 responded 'no', while a few answered: 'not aware', 'we did not notice', 'the athletes who get salaries are only at the World Cup level, therefore only one athlete is paid by the federation and it's sponsors', and 'we do focus on women's empowerment'. The latter statement, however, is difficult to interpret in relation to the question of financial support.

Table 3.2 Gender of national team athletes

Type of team	Male	Female	Total
Men and woman in different teams	7	1	8
Mixed team	152	85	237
Only men's team	16	N/A	16
Only women's team	N/A	0	0
Total	175	86	261

When it comes to introducing specific gender policies, the issue appears less important. Only 8 out of the 33 respondents answered 'yes' to the question of whether their organisation had one, and 5 elaborated on the content of the gender policy in place. Two of them answered 'equal treatment' and 'minimum two of five executive members should be female' – indicating that for these organisations, there are at least perceptions that there is gender equality. Another two were less clear in regard to their gender politics, stating: 'to fulfil wishes and requirements of women's sport' and 'the sports are different for ladies and boys'. With respect to the latter, it is interesting to note the use of the expression ladies versus boys, which may convey gendered connotations in itself.

One respondent, however, gave a more detailed description:

> Equal prices between sex categories in competitions, same equal competitions and formats for male and female riders, supporting female riders with their own snowboard event tour (Girls on Tour), trying to get at least one female judge in every competition, trying to have at least 3 female board members, 50% female and 50% male representatives in junior national team, aiming for equal gender ratio in employees (now it's 30% female, 70% male).

As shown in this statement, equality in competitions appears important, specifically in regard to the opportunities available and treatment of riders, as well as on the other side of the competition, in having a female judge, which may then relate to the criteria and perceptions of subjectivity in judging. In addition to this, supporting women by having their own event tour, in order to improve their snowboarding skills and be empowered in a women-only context. In regard to perspectives on gender equality then, equal representation is grounded in democratic ideals that should reflect the composition and rights of the entire population. In addition, special initiatives for females only tend to lead to perspectives that they are receiving 'preferential treatment', as for example used in relation to gender quotas, which may also have a stigmatising effect. Feminist scholars thus suggest shifting the focus from disadvantages of women to the extent of men's privilege (Bacchi, 2006).

Implications of gender-biased representation in snowboard organisations

In general, women are heavily under-represented in snowboarding organisations, and the higher up in the system – that is, from the national to the global – female representation seems to decrease. It is therefore worthwhile reflecting on what this means for the organisations' activities and regulations, as well as for the overall development of the sport. As noted by scholars in the field, the under-representation of women in sport leadership is so common that it often goes unnoticed, and when it is acknowledged, changes are slow to be implemented (Knoppers et al., 2019a).

Implications of this biased representation are best described through the term 'critical mass'. One of the first scholars to discuss gender balance in the context of organisations was Rosabeth Moss Kanter, in her book *Men and Women of the Corporation* (1977). Based on studies on gender dynamics in US-based corporations in the 1970s, she examined how access to opportunities and power impacted the behaviours and interactions of the organisations' employees. In the 1993 edition, she provided an updated picture of the corporate structure (Kanter, 1993), in which she highlighted how organisational structures determine the status of women, minorities (also impacting the lone man among women), and other excluded groups, and that an individual approach will not help ensure equality for the minority group. One of Kanter's central arguments revolves around how relative numbers of a dominant group versus a minority group will affect the behaviours and functioning of the whole organisation.

Kanter (1993) identified four group types defined by proportional representation of two social categories in the membership. *Uniform* groups have only one kind of person and can be considered homogenous, with respect to an external master status, such as sex, race or ethnicity, even though the group may go on to develop its own differentiations. *Skewed* groups are predominantly made up of one type of person, but with members of another group, usually up to a ratio of around 85:15. The type with the majority tend to control the group and its culture, while the few members belonging to a minority group are often treated as representatives of their category – as symbols rather than individuals. And, even if there are two tokens in such a group, it may be difficult for them to generate an alliance that could have any powerful influence within the group as a whole. *Titled* groups begin to move toward less extreme distributions, usually around 65:35 which may have less exaggerated effects. In this type of group, minority members may form potential allies and coalitions, and may have an influence on the total group. For the final type of group, that of a *balanced* group, this ratio is usually anywhere between 60:40 and 50:50, for which the interaction and culture reflect this balance.

Based on these four categories, Kanter discussed the possibilities of influence in relation to the various ratios, and suggested that the threshold or 'critical mass' – meaning the minimum number of individuals in the minority group required to have any power within the group as a whole – must measure at approximately one-third of the total number of group members. With reference to the composition of the executive boards for the organisations explored in this study as presented above, both the WSF and FIS are far from having women hold at least one-third of the executive positions. In the WSF and FIS, less than one-fourth of their representatives are women. The national organisations (combined, see Table 3.1) have about 20% women in the board positions. In comparison, analyses from the Sydney Scoreboard data (mentioned above) show that among the 45 countries included in the study, just one showed a gender balance in its board composition, and only four countries reached a critical mass of 30% (Adriaanse, 2016).

Following on from Kanter's original study based in a corporate context, the concepts of gender balance and critical mass are now used considerably in studies on public policy and governance, as well as in sport leadership research (e.g. Adriaanse, 2016, 2019). However, one might question the generalisation of applying the concept of critical mass to different kinds of organisations, as well as how the power dynamics within the corporate structure may hinder individual agency, which may not be the case in a different type of professional structure. For example, one could hypothesise that a contemporary organisation that represents snowboarders – a sport that emerged from the counterculture and anti-establishment philosophy, and which opposes traditional power structures – may be more open to (gender) diversity than more conventional organisations. I will next present a selection of results from my own research, on a study of a women's group within the Norwegian Snowboard Federation (NSBF), named the PowderPuff Girls (PPGirls). The results of this study may help illustrate the effect of individual/group engagement (Sisjord, 2013).

The PPGirls was established in 2003 and dissolved in 2012. It was initiated by three enthusiastic women, one of whom served as a member of the executive board for the NSBF, which consisted of one-third females at the time, but with a male president and a male vice-president. While practicing at various resorts, she had noticed very few women snowboarders compared to the number of men, and thus felt the need for there to be specific initiatives to involve more girls and women in the sport. She contacted two female snowboarders who were not members of the federation and they started planning how to proceed with activities and increase visibility. During its early phases, other people within the federation weren't really interested, and didn't notice their efforts. However, after a while, they gained acceptance for their work, and the group gradually expanded with support from the general secretary, who was a woman.

The group was not an official organisation and did not operate through memberships, however, rather it was perceived as a network with communication based on personal contacts and through a mailing list of associated PPGirls. A core group organised the activities, whom welcomed ideas and initiatives from other members of the PPGirls community. The group/network organised workshops and camps, and facilitated education for female coaches and competition judges. With support from the NSBF, they also arranged an international snowboard camp for women where they invited participants from other European countries. The camp was part of a larger project supported by the EU Youth Programme. An important goal for the PPGirls community was to increase women's representation on the NSBF executive board, which did, after a few years, increase to 50/50 for two periods, with the following three periods being led by a female president – who was, coincidentally, one of the founders of the PPGirls.

PPGirls played an important role in bringing gender issues onto the NSBF agenda. It is worth noting here, however, that the core members held central positions within the federation, on the board or in the administration, and were thus able to work towards integrating gender issues into the overall work carried out by the NSBF themselves. They succeeded in this for several years, but when the NSBF faced financial problems, the 'backing of females "became more a side thing" […] and more "important tasks" were given priority while the administrative staff was downsized' (Sisjord, 2013, p. 132), meaning that the number of administrative stuff was reduced. The impact of the core members' efforts also became visible when they eventually left their roles in the federation, and there were no 'new generation' in place to take over. The history of the PPGirls exemplifies the possibilities for individual and group efforts to make a change in the development of such organisations. On the other hand, this endeavour does also highlight the limitations of these initiatives when gender-equality policy is only weakly embedded within the existing organisational structure.

In order to actually achieve change in such sport organisations, it is important to look beyond proportional representation and organisational structures, and to include even more aspects, as suggested by Knoppers et al. (2019b). They identified several strategies for pinpointing the lack of gender diversity in sport governance, in which both discursive practices and the role of men and masculinity could apply to this context, and must be considered at the fore when researching such snowboarding organisations. The former strategy refers to assumptions of gender as a social construct and, how individuals create and develop meaning, including about gender. This approach requires a closer look at how people engage in practices of gender, and in so doing, sustain or challenge inequality. The other approach focuses on social hierarchies, specifically based on perceptions of masculinity and femininity. What is associated with desirable masculinity is usually valued more than what is associated with other forms of masculinity and femininity. For example, the desirable masculine practice may include participation in sports perceived as rigorous, competitive and requiring a great deal of physical and mental strength. Assumptions of men's superiority in these sports will naturally lead to men's dominance in the organisation, as well as prevailing perceptions of women as being less qualified. Thus, what is required when moving forward with such research and social initiatives is a holistic approach involving understandings of every level of the organisation, from its governance, to the context in which the organisation was founded, as well as the social dynamics occurring within its membership base. With this foundation, the sector would be in a much stronger place to tackle the gender inequality that still exists within the sport – from the top down.

References

Adriaanse, J.A. (2016). Gender diversity in the governance of sport associations: The Sydney Scoreboard Global Index of Participation. *Journal of Business Ethics, 137*(1), 149–160. DOI:10.1007/s10551-015-2550-3

Adriaanse, J.A. (2019). Europe in world perspective: The Sydney Scoreboard Global Index for women in sport leadership. In Elling, A., Hovden, J. & Knoppers, A. (Eds.), *Gender Diversity in European Sport Governance* (pp. 11–19). Routledge.

Bacchi, C. (2006). Arguing for and against quotas. In D. Dahlerup (Ed.), *Women, Quotas and Politics* (pp. 32–51). Routledge.

Elling, A., Knoppers, A. & Hovden, J. (2019). Meta-analysis. Data and methodologies. In Elling, A., Hovden, J. & Knoppers, A. (Eds.), *Gender Diversity in European Sport Governance* (pp. 179–191). Routledge.

Kanter, R.M. (1977). *Men and Women of the Corporation.* Basic Books.

Kanter, R.M. (1993). *Men and Women of the Corporation.* Basic Books.

Knoppers, A., Hovden, J. & Elling, A. (2019a). Introduction. In Elling, A., Hovden, J. & Knoppers, A. (Eds.), *Gender Diversity in European Sport Governance* (pp. 3–10). Routledge.

Knoppers, A., Hovden, J. & Elling, A. (2019b). Meta-analysis. Theoretical issues. In Elling, A., Hovden, J. & Knoppers, A. (Eds.), *Gender Diversity in European Sport Governance* (pp. 205–217). Routledge.

Rails. (2011). Project Rails: Reviewing and analyzing the international level of snowboarding. Master Dissertation, University of Oslo.

Sisjord, M.K. (2013). Women battling for a space in snowboarding. In Pfister, G. & Sisjord, M.K. (Eds.), *Gender and Sport: Changes and Challenges* (pp. 123–139). Waxmann Verlag.

Sisjord, M.K. (2019). Snowboarding: Women's agency from outsiders to insiders in the organisation. In Elling, A., Hovden, J. & A. Knoppers, A. (Eds.), *Gender Diversity in European Sport Governance* (pp. 165–175). Routledge and Taylor & Francis.

4 Snowboarding disciplines, facilities and injuries

The focus of this chapter will be on snowboarding styles and disciplines; snowboarding facilities and risks and injuries associated with the sport. First, I will give a short description of the main snowboarding disciplines. This will then be followed with a discussion on snowboarding facilities based on existing research in the field and interviews I conducted myself in connection with the present project. Thereafter, I will provide a review of the existing research on injuries prevalent among snowboarders. At the end of this section, I will highlight a number of issues concerning safeguarding and well-being.

Snowboarding styles, disciplines and competition formats

Snowboarding disciplines can be divided into two categories: the first being off-piste and backcountry snowboarding, which take place on terrain outside the boundaries of the ski resort (Reichenfeld & Bruechert, 1995), and the second being freestyle, typically performed in a snowboard park, and includes a number of styles, giving riders a choice of tricks and the versatility to pursue them. The types of event and competition vary, depending on the organiser. The most common include half-pipe, slopestyle, boardercross, and big air (Strittmatter et al., 2018; Thorpe, 2012). Alpine snowboarding is another major event, having been one of the first disciplines. The sport is also seeing a growing trend in hosting big mountain events. Below, you can find a description of the main disciplines based on definitions provided by Bakken et al. (2011), Batuev et al. (2020), Muñoz et al. (2018) and Teter and Schultz (2012).

Alpine snowboarding has a lot in common with alpine skiing. It is practiced on groomed pistes and focuses on carving linked turns. The formats for these competitions are slalom and giant slalom. Slalom is arranged in parallel runs with 20–35 pistes and may include up to three jumps. The vertical drop ranges from between 80 and 150 metres. The competition starts with qualification runs for which the participants run both pistes and the total time combined counts toward their ranking in the final competition. The giant slalom courses have 20–45 pistes, and a vertical drop of between 150 and 300 metres.

DOI: 10.4324/9781003007098-4

The participants compete on two runs, and the total time for both applies to their ultimate ranking. This discipline was introduced during the Olympic Games in Nagano, 1998.

Half-pipe (or superpipe, as it has become more commonly known in recent years) is one of the biggest events in snowboarding. Competitors perform tricks while in the air above the sides of the pipe as they ride from one side to the other. Riders are judged on overall performance, and those who receive highest scores are the athletes who attempt the most technical and difficult tricks. Managing to get good air when coming out of the pipe and being able to put a complete run together with different styles, will be awarded with higher scores. Half-pipe has been a part of the Olympic programme since 1998.

Boardercross (also known as Snowboard cross or Snowboard X) includes manoeuvring several jumps and obstacles while competing in heats, typically with four to six riders. The courses are quite narrow, and include cambered turns alongside both steep and flat sections, all designed to challenge the rider's ability to stay in control while maintaining maximum speed. Unlike other snowboard racing disciplines, such as giant slalom, the competitors ride on one single course together, at the same time. Boardercross has been included as an Olympic discipline since 2006.

Slopestyle combines the typical aspects of downhill snowboarding, including obstacles and big jumps, but with a long areal phase. The general slopestyle setup includes a few rails, followed by another rail or jib section, and ends with two or three jumps. There is usually a range of jibs to properly showcase different levels of skill and ability, as well as different features and jumps. Slopestyle events have a qualifying component held the day before the main event, where the riders are allowed two or three qualifying or seminal runs. Slopestyle was introduced to the Olympics during the Sochi Winter Games in 2014.

Big air contests consist of one massive jump, for which the rider performs one trick in the air with the aim to achieve significant height and distance, all while securing a clean landing. Competitors have two or three runs to land their best tricks, and the best one counts towards their final score. They are judged on amplitude, the trick itself, style, landing, and whether they can ride away clean. Big air is the most recent snowboarding event to be added to the Olympic programme, having been introduced in 2018 at the Beijing Olympics.

Big mountain has a lot in common with backcountry snowboarding, but was specifically developed into a competitive format. The events take place as more of a grassroots style competition, held on steeper, more advanced runs at specific resorts. Examples of this type of event include the Freeride World Tour, where both free-skiers and snowboarders participate. The focus for this type of snowboarding is on riding style, what's in front of you and how you handle the terrain. Judging is based on the riders' choice of line, how they ride the line, what tricks they perform, and how clean their run is. Enrolment is not required, and riders can participate as long as they enter the starting point before the limited number of slots fills up.

Snowboarding facilities – bigger and bigger

In regard to the size of snowboarding facilities, these have only continued to grow year on year. For example, in *Snowboard* (1995) Saga Areng and Martin Willners described half-pipes with pipe walls of 3–4 meters high. Today, the walls of the superpipes – those standard for international half-pipe competitions – measure in at '22 feet high', and elite-level slopestyle athletes may experience 'speeds up to 90 km per hour, jumping up to 30m in distance and up to 7m high' (Willmott & Collins, 2015, p. 1246).

The size of the facilities provided in snowboarding parks is an interesting topic given that they're used in competitions by both male and female riders, in contrast to many other sports, where adjustments are made with respect to the gender of those competing. For example, in ski jumping, women start from a higher level so that they can gain the speed men are able to get from a lower height, while in alpine skiing women and men actually compete on different courses altogether, with the main differentiation being for the super-giant slalom and downhill skiing competitions, correlating with potential challenges female athletes would face regarding the gates, jumps and speed. However, studies exploring the facilities themselves are limited in the scholarly research.

I have previously addressed this topic in two studies. The first in connection with a workshop organised by the Norwegian Snowboard Federation (NSBF) in October 2004. The second was conducted at a snowboarding camp in June 2006, also organised by the NSBF. Both studies draw on Bourdieu's conceptual work, with particular reference to types of capital – what kind of capital counts – and doxa, meaning *taken for granted* assumptions, which in the current case means *one size fits all*, with the one size referring to the design of facilities based on the male standard.

The first study (Sisjord, 2009) originated from a workshop I participated in as an observer. Following the workshop, I conducted qualitative interviews with some of the participants. While there were few men who attended, and who were involved with coaching and judging competitions, a majority of the participants were women. A central theme of the workshop was to discuss strategies that could help encourage more women to participate in snowboarding and motivate them to ride the half-pipe and big jumps. Reservations in attempting these were described among the women as coming from gender differences in *snowboarding self-esteem*. This presumably related to perceptions held by male riders about the female riders, as one of the interviewees commented: 'A lot of the boys are like: It's so boring to watch girls at the pipe, it's sooo boring'. The discussions within the workshop itself also focused on the fact that the nature of snowboarding facilities – that of being designed for male riders, and thus not ensuring optimal conditions for the female riders – may impact how others evaluate the female riders' performances, as one of the interviewees expressed:

> They use the same facilities, the same pipe, and that's a Monster-pipe. So, you can imagine; a girl with half the weight of a boy makes for quite different preconditions, which makes the level quite different. It looks bad, even if it's a good performance for a girl, she will always come short, visually, compared to the boys, who are flying up in the air, over the edge.
>
> (Sisjord, 2009, p. 1305)

When considering this statement in the perspective of Bourdieu's conceptualisation, this would indicate that women fall short in physical capital, which refers to understanding bodily expressions as possessing value in certain social fields, based on status and distinctive symbolic forms. The fact that women are offered the same facilities to compete on as men was thus explored from two different angles. One refers to the argument that other facilities should be provided to ensure female riders can perform to the best of their abilities, which they would likely be able to do on smaller pipes or jumps. It was noted that, with the situation as it stands, only a few dare to try and ride on the facilities on offer, and if they do, they can hardly perform their best tricks given the challenges they face in simply managing the jump at a sufficient speed. The other angle revolved around understanding that, if female athletes perform on facilities that haven't been designed with their needs in mind, they are at greater risk of sustaining an injury – for the big jumps in particular. Thus, the workshop participants debated what possibilities were available in order to introduce different sized jumps, admitting, however, that it might be a hard task to negotiate with resort owners on this, as they generally want to offer the 'best and biggest jumps' – the same issue being present with event organisers, who tend to want to book spectacular events and ensure significant publicity.

The second study (Sisjord, 2013) was conducted at the International Women's Snowboard Camp held at a summer ski resort in Southern Norway. The camp which lasted one week, was part of a broader project supported by the EU Youth Programme. The women's group within the NSBF, called the PowderPuff Girls, had invited other European countries to collaborate towards the promotion of women's snowboarding, focusing on: snowboarding in general, competitions, and network building to ensure future collaboration (see Sisjord, 2012). The camp attracted 20 female snowboarders from five European countries, including: Finland, Italy, Latvia, Norway and Sweden. Methods employed in the study were that of observation during the activities, followed by qualitative interviews with representatives from all participating countries.

In the invitation to the camp, it stated that there is a 'common understanding that girls are in need of girl-specific initiatives to increase involvement in snowboarding. For example, we should develop new competition formats for girls only and look into the possibility of adapting existing concepts for increased participation' (NSBF, 2006, p. 1). Hence, most of the interviews revolved around discussing the state of snowboarding facilities and competition formats in terms of the interviewees' personal experiences and perceptions/ ideas for alternative solutions.

The interviewees' narratives revealed significant variations regarding their positive and negative experiences, both in terms of personal outcome and the different levels of snowboarding they competed in that of local events to international contests. With respect to the facilities available and competition formats, the results of the interviews resonate with the main findings of my former study. Indeed, in the discussion of the potential constraints female snowboarders face when it comes to participating in competitions, several of the interviewees noted that the size of the half-pipes and big jumps were potential obstacles for them, as expressed by one interviewee as: 'Nowadays the problem is the size. Everything is getting so big, it's really tough. It may end up being too tough for females to participate' (Sisjord, 2013, p. 515). This issue was further discussed with reference to the risk of injury, and how women are more concerned about the consequences of an injury, and are therefore more likely to shy away from even attempting to participate when the jumps are too big. One of the interviewees, who had competed internationally, elaborated on this in reference to the half-pipes:

At first when I competed, the pipes were 3.5 metres high or so. That was fun. Now, I think super-pipes are about 5 to 6 metres high. We also tried some of those, but then it's really important that the pipes are in good shape. It's far easier to ride a well-shaped pipe. But, anyway, I think they are getting way too high, when considering participation by females.

(p. 515)

Two of the interviewees who used to participate in contests organised by the snowboard club took a slightly different position, confirming that in some instances, there were facilities specifically designed for female athletes, stating that: 'The girls have smaller jumps. You can, of course, choose the biggest one if you like, but almost nobody chooses it; we choose the small one'. This statement presumably only relates to the practice facilities though, as they further commented that: 'If there is a competition, there is always a kick-up for the girls and one for the guys' (p. 516). It should be noted, however, that their narratives generally indicated a relatively conservative view on gender dynamics, in which it was normal for the men to build the jumps for the women and would ask them: 'how big do you want it?'. This was an aspect that also highlighted variations in experiences in this context among participants from the different countries.

Snowboarding facilities were also discussed in a Swedish study (Pettersson & Wennberg-Olsson, 2015), based on qualitative interviews with a sample of female snowboarders and free-skiers. The study focused on: the reasons behind the lower rate of participation among women in both sports; what kind of opportunities and barriers girls and women commonly faced and whether the problems they experienced originated from the culture of the sport they participate in. The results revealed that there were in fact perceptions of a gender imbalance, namely stemming from physiological differences, that then meant that the height of both the jumps and the pipe wall became an obstacle for women who wanted to participate in the sport, with their findings also confirming that women are, on average, lighter than men and are consequently unable to achieve the same speed, and thus struggle to 'catch air' to perform the desired tricks. The authors concluded that facilities designed according to a male standard pose a challenge for the women and put them at risk of sustaining an injury.

In the interviews I conducted for the current project, the coaches and former elite snowboarders revealed various opinions of the issue. Most of them agreed that the facilities might be demanding for the female riders, but without really questioning it. Åshild Lofthus competed in slalom as her main discipline but also participated in the half-pipe given that both competition formats were combined in the final European Cup and Worlds Cups. Lofthus didn't have an issue with using the same facilities as the male snowboarders, which she explained as such:

No, I don't think so. It's not that we can't actually do it – it's more about the mind, mainly, [thinking] that we are not tough enough. You know, the guys are better at leaving their wits at the top [of the slope], whereas we have more barriers, I think a lot of it's to do with that, and, of course the physical aspects too.

She linked this assumption to gender differences, suggesting 'I think that we girls tend to analyse a lot more than the guys, don't you agree?'

Stine Brun Kjeldaas, whose main discipline was the half-pipe, explained her thoughts on the matter as follows:

Well, yes, I think they became very big over time, yes (laughter). But I never thought that we should ride on another pipe than the boys, no. You just have to learn to handle it, in a way. You see the girls today, they handle the huge pipes extremely well, so it's just a matter of trying to keep up, because you know, we were used to 4 metre high walls (…) but I remember the first super-pipes, and how they became bigger and bigger, and you just kind of had to try and learn to manage.

When I referred to the findings of the workshop (Sisjord, 2009) and that the participants confirmed that they thought the jumps were becoming too high for female riders, she responded: 'Yes, I can understand that, and for the big air and slopestyles, they're getting bigger and bigger and it's getting more dangerous, with more and bigger risks'. I followed up with a question on the recent developments within the sport, and whether that might impact the level of female participation, in the future, to which she answered:

> Well, when we see the girls riding today, they seem like they're able to handle it, so I think, in many ways it's good, that the girls ride the same [pipes and jumps] and can manage them. And the girls riding today, are riding on a much higher level than the guys did back when I used to compete, so they're managing to keep up. But I can understand that it might be difficult to, a bit more scary, to start, in a way.

Kjersti Buaas, the rider with the most varied experience in terms of disciplines and facilities used, seemed to echo Stine Brun Kjeldaas' perspective. In reference to the half-pipes, she had not noticed significant differences between the abilities of the female and male riders when it came to being able to ride the pipes, however, she did add that a lot depended on the riders' experience and former achievements. In her own words: 'If you've been riding for years, and you've gotten good at [riding] the pipes, then it doesn't really matter'. She further explained that it might be somewhat *mentally demanding* to come face to face with a 6 or 7 metre high wall, but once you get used to it, the bigger transition in the pipe felt almost safer than a smaller one, as the shape of the pipe appeared more decisive when it came to achieving what you set out to do, rather than the height of the walls. She didn't have anything to say about riding a smaller pipe either: 'It was not that I was scared of riding or that I had wanted a smaller pipe, I never thought that'.

Yet, in commenting on the jumps and slopestyle, she seemed to reveal somewhat of a different perspective. When discussing the jumps, it was apparently not an issue during practice, as one could choose between the sizes. In competitions, however, it might turn out to be more difficult, as she explained:

> It is a challenge to not get enough speed for a jump. You might end up on the flat [the flat section between the takeoff of the jump and the landing] and get injured. It's a scary feeling. And then, if you want to do a difficult trick, you can imagine that it could go really wrong if you don't have the speed you need and crash hard. In addition, if the conditions are icy, it's kind of like concrete, it does something to you mentally, right? And, most commonly, at least from my experience, that the jumps were made for the boys, and what they may be able to accomplish.

When she talked about slopestyle, she also commented on the jumps and speed. In regard to not achieving a fast enough speed – dependent on the weather and the quality of the snow – she noted that you have to be very focused on the jumps in order to get the best possible landing and then still gain enough speed for the next one. This was apparently the subject of a discussion among a few riders, however, it is often the case that some riders don't want to put off riding, despite the weather or quality of snow, for fear of being perceived as a wimp. She elaborates on this with an example of an incident during the X Games where she and two others – all well experienced or veteran riders, as she labelled them – suggested postponing the competition as it had started to snow. The other competitors – younger and less experienced – did not agree, most likely because sponsors were on site, as she indicated, and they had the organisers' support. The competition ended with the three veterans on the podium, as the only ones who had managed all of the jumps, while several of the other riders ended up injured. Even if she had been capable of handling the situation, she wasn't satisfied with her own performance, as she noted: 'You had to be aware of the conditions, and do more simple tricks, and then just about come over [the jumps], so then it's mainly about following procedure, right?'

Similar to Stine (as mentioned above), she also referred to the element of risk, and how the risk of sustaining an injury only increases when the facilities continue to get bigger and bigger. Additionally, she noted that the lack of opportunities for women to acquire and enhance their skills bothered her, which was mainly an issue when they were not given priority in the deciding on the size of the facilities. She provided an example of this happening in an event she called 'Nine Queens' that had been organised for female free-skiers and snowboarders, for which jumps were made with female participants in mind, and thus the event went particularly well, and the performance level of the athletes escalated significantly. With this example in mind, she emphasised the need to take both genders into account when designing new snowboarding facilities.

When I approached the national team coaches, both of their statements indicated that they conceded that the facilities may be more challenging for female riders. The statement provided by the senior team coach, however, was rather ambiguous:

> Both yes and no, usually it's OK. There are courses with huge jumps and courses with smaller jumps, so you just have to adjust. However, sometimes the jumps are in quite bad shape, and that makes it more difficult for the girls.

In regard to the latter, he mentioned the recent World Cup contest that had been arranged in a city – on a town square – with a jump and artificial scaffolding. The conditions were particularly bad, with several of the riders ending up injured, and as he said: 'It's mostly for entertainment, the sport doesn't gain anything, the performance level is lower and it's not optimal for the riders. And for those who are familiar with the sport, they are not happy about showcasing it this way'. As a general comment in response to the differences in gender and being able to manage difficult jumps, he believed that the males are often better at adjusting to the difficulties they might face.

When I discussed the facilities with the coach of the recruitment team, I asked whether the size of the facilities might be a barrier for female athletes' participation, providing a possible reason for why the rate of the said participation is lower among women, to which he answered:

> That may be right. We see it in the World Cups and European Cups and such, when it's one course that both guys and girls ride on, and some of the jumps can quickly get quite big. For example, in the Youth Olympic Games, before Covid -19 in 2020, the jump was enormous. The guys made it fairly well, even though they also struggled, but the girls were afraid of riding outside of the jump, and the level was particularly low. They weren't able to show what they were good at, in that instance. However, when they have a jump that they feel comfortable with, which they like, they do also send it [make a good jump with tricks]. So, it certainly is a barrier.

I followed up with a question regarding the differentiation in jumps and whether that has been an issue, to which he answered: 'Oh yes, it has, or there are always discussions about that, but it always ends up being about finances, how much one should put into it, maybe'. He further explained that in the European Cup, compared to the World Cup, the courses used to be a bit smaller in size 'so that may help the girls a bit', indicating an understanding that there are challenging rides for the females.

The secondary school coaches had different experiences with this than the elite coaches and former elite snowboarders, mostly relating to differentiation in practice between genders in the school lesson, and that of regional competitions and Norway Cup events. The two coaches also verbalised different perceptions of the issue. When I asked the female coach about her opinion on equal facilities for both genders, her immediate answer was:

> Yes, for that, I have changed my mind over the years. By now I think, at the top level internationally, when you see the Olympic Games now, that's another thing. But if you're looking at the Olympic Games, or maybe the European Cup, and World Cup for that matter, I think it's better with smaller courses or smaller jumps, smaller elements, to see better tricks, compared to when they have to ride the guy's course, if you can call it. And probably making tricks at a skill level beneath what they're actually able to do, because they don't dare try it, or because the risk is too high, and for good reason. And especially when we talk about the club and national level, to get more female riders involved.

When I followed up on this and asked why she had changed her mind, she said that, formerly, she had thought that you shouldn't make concessions, or make things different for female athletes, that you just had to get on with it, but added that since then, she had possibly 'become more mature and grown up'. Furthermore, she argued that the audience for such events would be able to enjoy the accomplishments of the female athletes, for example when a rider made a '1080 instead of a fiver or a seven, that's much more fun to watch' meaning that seeing the complexity of the trick is more impressive than the height of the jumps.

The male coach had a different point of view. He related the proposal for a differentiation in facilities for male and female riders as an issue primarily connected to skill enhancement and did not distinguish between what female and male riders were capable of achieving. In elaborating on the issue, he was most concerned with the students at the school and the national level and said he was not much involved with international standards.

The size of the facilities has also received much public attention, with noteworthy examples of this seen in the debates surrounding the World Championship held in Oslo, Norway, in 2012. The following was published on P3, a channel owned by the Norwegian Broadcasting Corporation. One of the world's best snowboarders at the time, Torstein Horgmo (Norway) expressed his opinion as follows: 'It's obvious. The girls should've had another course', meaning that he understood that the slopestyle course was built for the male riders, and most of the female athletes were not suited for the giant World Cup course. The organiser responded: 'Nobody wants to use small jumps'.

Horgmo further argued that most of the female riders struggled to get over the jumps in the way they needed to, which resulted in their not picking up enough speed', and making hard landings. In his opinion, women's slopestyle could be much more spectacular if they had their own jumps for major contests such as the World Cup, and which could easily be made on a smaller scale near the huge facilities. He referred to the accomplishments of the gold and silver medal winners, noting that: 'Spencer O'Brien and Jamie Anderson are in a separate division, in any case' and continued: 'Kjersti [Buaas] is probably the next on that list, but with smaller jumps, more riders could push their own boundaries, in terms of tricks. Instead, they're having to lower their limits to tackle large and icy jumps'.

The 2012 bronze medal winner, Enni Ruukajärvi, agreed with Horgmo in that only a few women in elite snowboarding could manage jumps like that, but also stated, however, that she would not be interested in a separate course for women: 'No, I prefer to ride under the same conditions as the guys'. It should be noted that the referred publication received significant responses from the public, most of them supporting one course for both genders.

Injuries in snowboarding

The growth in the popularity of snowboarding has been accompanied with an increased number of studies into snowboarding-related injuries, particularly in the field of the medical sciences. These range from small case studies to large database studies with thousands of registered injuries having been compiled from all over the world (Bladin et al., 2004). A growing number of studies have explored the prevalence of different types of injuries in light of various different variables, such as gender, age and skill level, and riding conditions. In general, the most common injuries occur in the upper-extremity, shoulder and the head resulting in fractures, sprains, strains or concussions, mainly caused by falls or collisions. Injuries in the torso and lower extremities appear less prevalent, although this seems to vary depending on skill level.

Research in the field covers both recreational snowboarding and elite sport. These studies tend to be based either solely on snowboarders or on samples of downhill skiers and snowboarders, and conducted as single case studies as well as meta-studies. Some studies report on gender differences, while others include female and male riders in the sample but without reference to gender difference in the analysis, while some studies do not mention the gender of the participants at all. In the following section, I will highlight some of the research relevant to this book. The intention is not to give a comprehensive overview of the literature, meaning that details about the injuries and the prevalence of the type of injury has been omitted, rather I will provide an outline of the research based on samples from the main databases and ski resorts (such as ski patrol accident reports), medical clinics and so on, and then the same for the studies from international competitions.

General trends in snowboarding injuries

There is evidence that the risk of severe injuries is higher in terrain parks than on regular slopes (Audet et al., 2019; Hosaka et al., 2020; Stenroos, 2018; Torjussen & Bahr, 2006). Empirical findings indicate a variation in injuries from discipline to discipline, where the risk of injury is higher in snowboard cross and big air, than for the half-pipe (Torjussen & Bahr, 2005).

The level of performance appears to impact the risk of injury as well, however, there appears to be conflicting evidence. Some studies report a higher risk of injury among younger and/or less experienced snowboarders (Audet et al., 2019; Coury et al., 2013; DeFroda et al., 2016; Dickson & Terwiel, 2011; Idzikowski et al., 2000; Sulheim et al., 2011). While other studies correlated the types of injury to the riders' increased skill level, for example, as in a study by Ogawa et al. (2010) that found that regions of the trunk and multiple injuries increased in line parallel to one's skill level, while upper extremity injuries decreased.

With respect to gender, the empirical findings are also somewhat conflicting. Several studies reported a greater number of injuries and, on the whole, more serious injuries among male riders than among female riders (Audet et al., 2019; Basques et al., 2018; DeFroda et al., 2016; De Roulet et al., 2017; Girardi et al., 2010; Idzikowski et al., 2000; Weinstein et al., 2019). Other studies reported more injuries among female snowboarders, although this was commonly in combination with younger and less experienced riders (Bladin et. al., 2004; Kim et al., 2012; Russell & Selci, 2018). Additionally, a few studies reported no gender differences in snowboarding injuries (Bissel et al., 2008; Hasler et al., 2010; Torjussen & Bahr, 2006). In general, gender differences are not discussed in the research, except for in the study conducted by Idzikowski et al. (2000) who suggested that it was more common to see more of an aggressive riding style among male riders, similarly to that found in the study carried out by De Roulet et al. (2019) who highlighted a greater level of risk-taking among younger, male participants.

Studies from international competitions

A few studies examined injuries sustained during the Olympic Games and World Cup competitions. Engebretsen et al. (2010) analysed the frequency and characteristics of injuries and illnesses during the Olympic Games in Vancouver (2010). The risk of sustaining an injury was highest for bobsleigh, ice hockey, short track, alpine freestyle and snowboard cross, whereas the incidence of injuries was higher in female athletes than it was for their male counterparts. The results on injuries per gender do not distinguish between disciplines, but the risk of injury in freestyle and snowboard cross was emphasised and explained by the speed commonly required to succeed in these sports, combined with external factors such as challenges with the turns, jumps and waves, on top of competing in one, joint heat alongside other riders.

There were a number of studies based on the Olympic Games in Sochi (2014) that also focused on injuries and illnesses. Soligard et al. (2015) reported that, altogether, 12% of the athletes incurred at least one injury. The percentage was highest in aerial skiing, snowboard slopestyle, snowboard cross, slopestyle skiing, half-pipe skiing, moguls skiing, alpine skiing and snowboard half-pipe. In this study, the injury rate among female and male athletes was quite similar, except for the fact that female athletes were at a significantly higher risk of injury when it came to slopestyle skiing. In comparison, a study conducted by Palmer-Green and Elliott (2015), focusing on the British team, reported that 39% of the athletes sustained at least one injury. The risk of injury was highest for freestyle skiing, skeleton and snowboarding, and slightly higher among female athletes (44%) than males (36%) – although this was not statistically significant.

The Youth Olympic Games, for athletes aged 14–18 years, was introduced in 2012 and held in Innsbruck, Austria. Out of the 1021 registered athletes (45% of whom were women, and 55% were men), a total of 111 injuries were reported. The injury frequency varied substantially between sports, with the highest ones in half-pipe skiing and snowboarding half-pipe and slopestyle. On average, there was a slightly higher incidence of injuries among the male athletes, but this was not statistically significant (Ruedl et al., 2012).

Studies of World Cup competitions also looked into patterns of injury among freestyle skiers and/or snowboarders. With respect to snowboarding disciplines, Torjussen and Bahr (2005) reported a high risk of injury for big air, snowboard cross, and half-pipe, while the risk of injury for the snowboard slalom disciplines was lower. Comparable findings were reported by Major et al. (2014). Yet again, none of these studies reported on gender differences. In comparison, however, there are other studies that did report on gender differences in their research, but they all contradict each other. Steenstrup et al. (2011) analysed injuries in qualifications compared to the final runs in snowboard cross and ski cross. The injury incidence was significantly higher in final runs compared to the qualification runs for males participating in the snowboard cross competitions, but not for their female counterparts and nor for the ski cross riders. The authors correlated the results to external factors such as space constraints on the course and competition for the ideal line, but provided no further explanation to this. Another study focusing on head injuries reported that freestyle skiers had the highest overall head injury incidence, followed by snowboarders and alpine skiers. Across all three disciplines, the incidence was higher in female athletes than in the male athletes (Steenstrup et al., 2014).

In regard to comparing the conflicting findings in recreational as well as professional snowboarding, one should be aware of methodological limitations in the research. Common methodological issues in all alpine/ski sports are that case ascertainment is problematic and the accurate measurement of exposure is limited, for example, when injured riders avoid medical attention and thereby not being included in the studies (Bladin et al, 2004). Another issue in the proportion of female vs. male athlete. Many of the studies rely on samples of injured riders, and as male riders make up the majority of snowboarders, it can be expected that the male athletes will outnumber the female athletes in the statistics. A meta-analysis by Audet et al. (2019) reported that the odds of finding a male rider on the slopes, compared to that of finding a female rider, were four to eight times higher in terrain parks than on regular slopes. This suggests an interaction between the higher risk of injuries in terrain parks (as mentioned above) and the number of male participants. Torjussen and Bahr (2005) on the other hand, registered incidence of injury per 1.000 runs, based on a study of athletes competing in national championships in Norway. The results revealed more injuries among the female riders, particularly for the big jump competitions; however, this was not statistically comparable due to the relatively small number of injuries.

As gender has been paid little attention in the research presented here, and if – as only one among other variables, it is worth to include results from a Bachelor thesis that focused on injuries in slopestyle, and gender differences with particular attention to knee injuries (Buaas, 2014). The study was developed by four former elite athletes in skiing and snowboarding slopestyle. The sample was based on ranking lists from the World Snowboard Tour, the Winter

X Games, and the Winter Dew Tour for the 2009–2010 season. The athletes ranked in the top 100 were invited to participate in an online survey, of which women and men were equally represented. The main question was: 'Have you ever had a serious injury at a slopestyle competition? Serious injury was defined as *kept you out of action for three months or more*. The results showed that 68% women and 37% men answered 'yes'. Among the injured riders, 63% of the women and 29% of the men answered that they had sustained knee injuries. A central issue in the study revolved around the jumps (including their size), and the results showed that 92% of the women, and 64% of the men said that their injury was a result of the jumps (compared to other features). It should be noted that the author, Kjersti Buaas, is one of the featured professional snowboarders in this book, also cited above in this chapter.

Safeguarding and well-being

In general, books about snowboarding tend to cover topics like styles and disciplines, technique, equipment, clothing and caring for the snowboard, but they also commonly include a chapter on safety (Areng & Willners, 1995; Reichenfeld & Bruechert, 1995; Teter & Schultz, 2012). For backcountry snowboarding, knowledge of avalanches (temperature, snow conditions and snow profiles) and equipment are of great importance. For snowboarding in resorts and terrain parks, safety is mostly related to one's equipment, practicing safe behaviour on the slopes, and pre-snowboarding fitness programmes and recommendations for training. The most common items for protection are wrist guards, padding/back protection and helmets.

The scientific research on this subject has predominantly focused on the use of helmets, seeing as head injuries are the most frequent reason for hospital admission in the sport, and the most common cause of serious injury and death (Sulheim et al., 2006). The use of a helmet has been an issue from as far back as when snowboarding began to enter the mainstream, which was influenced by, and discussed in connection with, the use of helmets in other sports, with the most relevant here being downhill skiing. Discussions have revolved around the potential benefits and recommendations, and of mandatory equipment in competitions. Helmets have been proposed as an injury-prevention strategy, yet their protective value remains the subject of intense debate (Cusimano & Kwok, 2010). Those opposing the use of helmets have even gone as far as to claim that helmets may increase the risk of injury, because they may lead to impaired hearing, a reduced field of vision, or increased speed through a false feeling of security and thus increase the incidence of collisions – the cause of many severe injuries in the sport. Another argument relates to the uncertainty about whether it may cause a risk of neck and cervical spine injuries, as a result of a guillotine effect due to the heavy helmet (Sulheim et al., 2006).

In regard to what the research says on this topic, Cusimano and Kwok (2010) conducted a systematic review of the effectiveness of wearing a helmet among skiers and snowboarders. Based on the inclusion criteria, the analysis included ten studies of varying designs and results. The authors concluded with strong evidence to support the protective value of helmets in reducing the risk of injury, however, they found no evidence to support the claim that the use of helmets may lead to a higher risk of cervical spine injuries or neck injuries. The review study does not mention gender/sex differences, nor is it a focus in the presentation of the studies they included.

Sulheim et al. (2017) reported on three different studies based on skiers and snowboarders in terrain parks. The aim of the study was to determine the effect of the expected increase in the amount of people wearing helmets over a certain time span, relating to the recommendation of helmet use. The results revealed that helmet use was associated with improved odds for avoiding head injuries, and especially serious injuries. Gender (male/female/unknown) was only mentioned in the samples in terms of demographics, together with age and nationality, but otherwise, this was not further discussed. This seems to be the general trend across the research on injuries mentioned above, which may indicate that gender has been of minor importance in the focus of this area of research.

References

Areng, S. & Willners, M. (1995). *Snowboard.* Rabén & Sjögren.

Audet, O., Hagel, B.E., Nettel-Aguirre, A., Mitra, T., Emery, C.A., Macpherson, A., Lavoie, M.D. & Goulet, C. (2019). What are the risk factors for injuries and injury prevention strategies for skiers and snowboarders in terrain parks and half-pipes? A systematic review. *British Journal of Sports Medicine, 53*(1), 19–24. DOI:10.1136/bjsports-2018-099166

Bakken, A., Bere, T., Bahr, R., Kristianslund, E. & Nordsletten, L. (2011). Mechanisms of injuries in World Cup snowboard cross: A systematic video analysis of 19 cases. *British Journal of Sports Medicine, 45,* 1315–1322. DOI:10.1136/bjsports-2011-090527

Basques, B.A., Gardner, E.C., Samuel, A.M., Webb, M.L., Lukasiewicz, A.M., Bohl, D.D. & Grauer, J.N. (2018). Injury patterns and risk factors for orthopaedic trauma from snowboarding and skiing: A national perspective. *Knee Surgery, Sports Traumatology, Arthroscopy, 26*(7), 1916–1926. DOI:10.1007/s00167-016-4137-7

Batuev, M., Zipp, S. & Robinson, L. (2020). Snowboarding and skateboarding. In J. Nauright & S. Zipp (Eds.), *Routledge Handbook of Global Sport* (pp. 446–463). Routledge.

Bissel, B.T., Johnson, R.J., Shafritz, A.B., Chase, D.C. & Ettlinger, C.F. (2008). Epidemiology and risk factors of humerus fractures among skiers and snowboarders. *The American Journal of Sports Medicine, 36*(10), 1880–1888. DOI:10.1177/0363546508318195

Bladin, C., McCrory, P. & Pogorzelski, A. (2004). Snowboarding injuries. Current trends and future directions. *Sports Medicine, 34*(2), 133–139. 0112–1642/04/0002–0133/$31.00/0

Buaas, K. (2014). *The Other Side of the Gold Medal. Bachelor Thesis in Physical Education and Sports Studies.* (Unpublished). Høgskolen in Nord-Trøndelag.

Coury, T., Napoli, A.M., Wilson, M., Daniels, J., Murray, R. & Milzman, D. (2013). Injury patterns in recreational alpine skiing and snowboarding at a mountainside clinic. *Wilderness & Environmental Medicine, 24*(4), 417–421. DOI:10.1016/j.wem.2013.07.002

Cusimano, M.D. & Kwok, J. (2010). The effectiveness of helmet wear in skiers and snowboarders: A systematic review. *British Journal of Sports Medicine, 44,* 781–796. DOI:10.1136/bjsm.2009.070573

DeFroda, S.F., Gil, J.A. & Owens, B.D. (2016). Epidemiology of lower extremity injuries presenting to the emergency room in the United States: Snow skiing vs. snowboarding. *Injury, 47*(10), 2283–2287. DOI:10.1016/j.injury.2016.07.005

De Roulet, A., Inaba, K., Strumwasser, A., Chouliaras, K., Lam, L., Benjamin, E., Grabo, D. & Demetriades, D. (2017). Severe injuries associated with skiing and snowboarding: A national trauma data bank study. *The Journal of Trauma and Acute Care Surgery, 82*(4), 781–786. DOI:10.1097/TA.0000000000001358

Dickson, T.J. & Terwiel, F. A. (2011). Snowboarding injuries in Australia: Investigating risk factors in wrist fractures to enhance injury prevention strategies. *Wilderness & Environmental Medicine, 22*(3), 228–235. DOI:10.1016/j.wem.2011.04.002

Engebretsen, L., Steffen, K., Alonso, J.M., Aubry, M., Dvorak, J., Junge, A., Meeuwisse, W., Mountjoy, M., Renström, P. & Wilkinson, M. (2010). Sports injuries and illnesses during the Winter Olympic Games 2010. *British Journal of Sports Medicine, 44*(11), 772–780. DOI:10.1136/bjsm.2010.076992

Girardi, P., Braggion, M., Sacco, G., De Giorgi, F. & Corra, S. (2010). Factors affecting injury severity among recreational skiers and snowboarders: An epidemiology study. *Knee Surgery, Sports Traumatology, Arthroscopy: Official Journal of the ESSKA, 18*(12), 1804–1809. DOI:10.1007/s00167-010-1133-1

Hasler, R.M., Berov, S., Benneker, L., Dubler, S., Spycher, J., Heim, D., Zimmermann, H. & Exadaktylos, A.K. (2010). Are there risk factors for snowboard injuries? A case-control multicentre study of 559 snowboarders. *British Journal of Sports Medicine, 44*(11), 816–821. DOI:10.1136/bjsm.2010.071357

Hosaka, N., Arai, K., Otsuka, H. & Kishimoto, H. (2020). Incidence of recreational snowboarding-related spinal injuries over an 11-year period at a ski resort in Niigata, Japan. *BMJ Open Sport & Exercise Medicine, 6,* e000742. DOI:10.1136/bmjsem-2020-000742

Idzikowski, J.R., Janes, P.C. & Abbott, P.J. (2000). Upper extremity snowboarding injuries. Ten-year results from the Colorado snowboard. *The American Journal of Sports Medicine, 28*(6), 825–832. DOI:10.1177/03635465000280061001

Kim, S., Endres, N.K., Johnson, R.J., Ettlinger, C.F. & Shealy, J.E. (2012). Snowboarding injuries: Trends over time and comparisons with alpine skiing injuries. *The American Journal of Sports Medicine, 40*(4), 770–776. DOI:10.1177/0363546511433279

Major, D.H, Steenstrup, S.E., Bere, T., Bahr, R. & Nordsletten, L. (2014). Injury rate and injury pattern among elite World Cup snowboarders: A 6-year cohort study. *British Journal of Sports Medicine, 48,* 18–22. DOI:10.1136/bjsports-2013-092573

Muñoz, J., Garcia-Rubio, J., Ramos, D., León, K. & Collado-Mateo, D. (2018). Effects of jump difficulty on the final performance in snowboard-slopestyle-winter Olympic Games, Socchi, 2014. *Annals of Applied Sport Science, 6*(2), 15–21. DOI:10.29252/aassjournal.6.2.15

Norwegian Broadcasting Corporation. https://arkiv.p3.no/snobrett/index.html@p=2039.html

Norwegian Snowboard Federation (NSBF). (2006). *International Snowboard Summer Camp for Girls. Invitation.* Oslo: Norges Snowboardforbund.

Ogawa H., Sumi, H., Sumi, Y. & Shimizu, K. (2010). Skill level-specific differences in snowboarding-related injuries. *The American Journal of Sports Medicine, 38*(3), 532–537. DOI:10.1177/0363546509348763

Palmer-Green, D. & Elliott, N. (2015). Sports injury and illness epidemiology: Great Britain Olympic Team (TeamGB) surveillance during the Sochi 2014 Winter Olympic Games. *British Journal of Sports Medicine, 49*(1), 25–29. DOI:10.1136/bjsports-2014-094206

Pettersson, J.H. & Wennberg-Olsson, L. (2015). 'Killar kommer alltid vara bättre, så är livet att vara tjej': En kvalitativ undersökning om kvinnors plats inom sporterna snowboard och freeskiing ['The guys will always do better', that's life as a girl': A qualitative study about women's place in the sports of snowboarding and freeskiing]. Idrottsvetenskapliga programmet, Pedagogiska institutionen [The Sport Science Programme. Institute of Education]. University of Umeå.

Reichenfeld, R. & Bruechert, A. (1995). *Snowboarding.* Human Kinetics.

Ruedl, G., Schobersberger, W., Pocecco, E., Blank, C., Engebretsen, L., Soligard, T., Steffen, K., Kopp, M. & Burtscher, M. (2012). Sport injuries and illnesses during the first Winter Olympic Games 2012 in Innsbruck, Austria. *British Journal of Sports Medicine, 46*(15), 1030–1037. DOI:10.1136/bjsports-2012-091534

Russell, K. & Selci, E. (2018). Pediatric and adolescent injury in snowboarding. *Research in Sports Medicine, 26*(Sup1), 166–185. DOI:10.1080/15438627.2018.1438277

Sisjord, M.K. (2009). Fast-girls, babes and the invisible girls. Gender relations in snowboarding. *Sport in Society, 12*(10), 1299–1316. DOI:10.1080/17430430903204801

Sisjord, M.K. (2012). Networking among women snowboarders: A study of participants at an international snowboard camp. *Scandinavian Journal of Medicine and Science in Sports, 22*, 73–84. DOI:10.1111/j.1600-0838.2010.01135.x

Sisjord, M.K. (2013). Women's snowboarding. Some experiences and perceptions of competitions. *Leisure Studies, 32*(5), 507–523. DOI:10.1080/02614367.2012.685334

Soligard, T., Steffen, K., Palmer-Green, D., Aubry, M., Grant, M.-E., Meeuwisse, W., Mountjoy, M., Budgett, R. & Engebretsen, L. (2015). Sports injuries and illnesses in the Sochi 2014 Olympic Winter Games. *British Journal of Sports Medicine, 49*(7), 441–447. DOI:10.1136/bjsports-2014-094538

Steenstrup, S.E., Bere, T. & Bahr, R. (2014). Head injuries among FIS World Cup alpine and freestyle skiers and snowboarders: A 7-year cohort study. *British Journal of Sports Medicine, 48*, 41–45. DOI:10.1136/bjsports-2013-093145

Steenstrup, S.E, Bere, T., Flørenes, T.W., Bahr, R. & Nordsletten, L. (2011). Injury incidence in qualification runs versus final runs in FIS World Cup snowboard cross and ski cross. *British Journal of Sports Medicine, 45*(16), 1310–1314. DOI:10.1136/bjsports-2011-090528

Stenroos, A. (2018). *Alpine Sports Injuries in Finland: A Retrospective Analysis of Skiing and Snowboarding Injuries.* Academic Dissertation. Department of Orthopaedics and Traumatology Helsinki University Hospital and University of Helsinki, Faculty of Medicine, Helsinki. http://urn.fi/URN:ISBN:978-951-51-4158-3

Strittmatter, A.-M., Kilvinger, B., Bodemar, A., Skille, E. & Kurscheidt, M. (2018). Dual governance structures in action sports: Institutionalization processes of professional snowboarding revisited. *Sport in Society, 22*(19), 1655–1673. DOI:10.1080/17430437.2018.1440696

Sulheim, S., Ekeland, A., Holme, I. & Bahr, R. (2017). Helmet use and risk of head injuries in alpine skiers and snowboarders: Changes after an interval of one decade. *British Journal of Sports Medicine, 51*, 44–50. DOI:10.1136/bjsports-2015-095798

Sulheim, S., Holme, I., Ekeland, A. & Bahr, R. (2006). Helmet use and risk of head injuries in alpine skiers and snowboarders. *JAMA, 295*(8), 919–924. DOI:10.1001/jama.295.8.919

Sulheim, S., Holme, I., Rødven, A., Ekeland, A. & Bahr, R. (2011). Risk factors for injuries in alpine skiing, telemark skiing and snowboarding – Case-control study. *British Journal of Sports Medicine, 45*(16), 1303–1309. DOI:10.1136/bjsports-2011-090407

Teter, H. & Schultz, T. (2012). *Mastering Snowboarding*. Champaign, IL: Human Kinetics.

Thorpe, H. (2012). *Snowboarding: The Ultimate Guide*. Greenwood Press.

Torjussen, J. & Bahr, R. (2005). Injuries among competitive snowboarders at the national elite level. *The American Journal of Sports Medicine, 33*(3), 370–377. DOI:10.1177/0363546504268043

Torjussen, J. & Bahr, R. (2006). Injuries among elite snowboarders (FIS Snowboard World Cup). *British Journal of Sports Medicine, 40*(3), 230–234. DOI:10.1136/bjsm.2005.021329

Weinstein, S, Khodaee, M. & VanBaak, K. (2019). Common skiing and snowboarding injuries. *Current Sports Medicine Reports, 18*(11), 394–400. DOI:10.1249/SR.0000000000000651

Willmott, T. & Collins, D. (2015). Challenges in the transition to mainstream: Promoting progress and minimizing injury in freeski and snowboarding. *Sport and Society, 18*(10), 1245–1259. DOI:10.1080/17430437.2015.1031530

5 Training and coaching in snowboarding

The focus of this chapter is on training and coaching – a broad field in scientific terms, as it encompasses perspectives from both the natural sciences and the social sciences. This means that to be a coach requires extensive knowledge of anatomy and physiology as well as psychology, pedagogy, and sociology, all of which serve as a foundation for being able to teach and facilitate an athlete's skill acquisition, injury prevention and the avoidance of overtraining (P.E. Robinson, 2010). It is, however, beyond the scope of this chapter to delve into these various fields separately – instead then I shall refer to them when discussing issues related to snowboarding and gender in regard to current explorations of these topics in the body of research. Thus, I shall include a section dedicated to the physical requirements of the sport, of which are rooted in the natural science tradition, before, briefly commenting on coaching as a gendered profession. Thereafter, I shall concentrate on training and coaching in snowboarding, focusing specifically on the gender differences that currently exist in the sport.

Coaching in snowboarding is a topic that has only recently been discussed in the field of research, something that can mainly be attributed to the nature and organisation of the sport, and its history of being 'anti-competition' and its 'do it yourself' philosophy, of which the participants themselves were perceived to be the experts and innovators of the sport. Indeed, who exactly could they learn from? And, as in other actions sports, the use of a coach was considered antithetical to the counter-culture philosophy at its core (Thorpe & Dumont, 2019). As a result of the eventual institutionalisation, commercialisation and professionalisation of the sport, however, snowboarders have taken after more traditional sports in regard to the use of training strategies and utilising various kinds of expertise, such as that of exercise physiologists and psychologists.

With respect to gender issues and coaching in snowboarding, I have not come across any studies that specifically explore this topic. Because of this, I will solely rely on the interviews with the coaches first presented in the introduction to this book as a basis for my exploration of the subject, and the focus of this chapter will thus mainly be spent elaborating on and examining the coaches' experiences of coaching both female and male snowboarders.

DOI: 10.4324/9781003007098-5

Physical requirements

As a result of the institutionalisation and professionalisation of snowboarding of recent years the sport has increasingly attracted the interest of exercise physiologists and sport scientists (Vernillo et al., 2018). Much attention has been devoted to the athletes' physical profiles and physiological and biomechanical requirements – aspects that sports scientists and strength and conditioning coaches may need to consider when working with these types of athletes in particular (Turnbull et al., 2011). Most of this research has examined elite snowboarders, commonly those competing for national teams or participants at international competitions such as the Olympic Games. Some studies have focused on specific disciplines, such as boardercross (Gathercole et al., 2015; Smith et al., 2015), half-pipe (Turnbull et al., 2011), alpine snowboarding (Vernillo et al., 2017), and several other combinations of disciplines (Platzer et al., 2009; Vernillo et al., 2016a). Other studies describe 'snowboarders' as the sample unit without defining the specific discipline (Jeon & Eom, 2021; Zebrowska et al., 2012). A few studies focus specific on riding positions, such as the evaluation of laterality in the basic snowboarding position (Staniszewski et al., 2016) and strength asymmetry between the front and rear legs (Vernillo et al., 2016b).

This overview gives an illustration of a growing interest in the field. However, as aforementioned, it is worth noting that issues of gender are hardly touched upon. Some studies are based on both female and male participants, while other studies include men only. In cases where gender is mentioned, this usually only relates to differentiations in test scores and/or parameters. For example, Smith et al. (2015) reported height and weight, leg power, leg endurance and core endurance among male and female participants, where it was found that men had, on average, higher scores than women. Another study aimed at assembling and evaluating a battery of tests for the snowboard disciplines of parallel, cross, big air and half-pipe (Platzer et al., 2009). The test battery comprised tests for aerobic capacity, balance, jumping, isokinetic core power, leg power, bench press, bench pulls and a snowboard start simulator. With respect to gender, the study showed that the test battery predicted better for woman than for men, but this was not elaborated on with further discussions.

Coaching – a gendered profession

Coaching is a male-dominated domain, in several ways. First, men make up the majority of coaches. In fact, the higher the athlete's performance level, the more likely it is they will be coached by a male coach (Acosta & Carpenter, 2014; Demers, 2009; Fasting et al., 2017; Pfister, 2013). It is important to note, however, that this skewed gender ratio does vary from country to country as well as across sport disciplines (Robertson, 2016).

Along with a growth in the coaching profession as a whole, a lot of studies have explored the development of coaching expertise and pathways into coaching based on the coaches' own athletic performance level and/or in combination with any coaching education they may have. Yet, these studies also appear to be 'gender blind' in terms of their research questions as well as the samples included (for an overview, see Sisjord et al., 2021). Furthermore, the gender bias has an impact on coaching education and curricula, where males commonly are perceived and presented as the 'normal' athlete while females are denoted as 'the other' (Alsarve, 2018; Grahn, 2014), or female athletes may only be included in entirely about coaching female athletes specifically (Etnier, 2011; LaVoi et al., 2007). Scholarly research has examined the coaching of girls/women versus boys/men. For example, Norman (2016) made a review of former studies that showed differences in communication, coaching styles, personal relationships, differences in motivation levels when it came to participation, and the coaches' perceptions of the different needs of the athletes in regard to receiving feedback and encouragement between female and male athletes. Other studies have focused on high-performance female athletes and their experiences of the coach–athlete relationship, which is most commonly with a male coach (Hovden & Tjønndal, 2019; Norman, 2015; Norman & French, 2013).

Following the increase in alternative sports, risk sports and the like (see concepts mentioned in the introductory chapter), recent research has paid attention to the various aspects related to learning and coaching. Many activities exist in the realm of the wider field of 'outdoor sports', where one practices the sport in natural environments, and which are commonly perceived as challenging in terms of accomplishment. Collins and Collins (2012, 2013) discuss the use of the term 'coach' in generic terms as opposed to the concepts 'guide', 'instructor' and 'teacher'. They refer to activities such as mountaineering, rock climbing, sea kayaking and white water kayaking – all characterised by a certain degree of risk, in that they possess an element of physical challenge and require specific technical skills.

Other studies focus more closely on the role of the coach, such as the coaches' use of interpersonal strategies, tools and techniques with regard to how and the extent to which they influence the participants' actions and behaviours (Gray & Collins, 2016), and how the coaches perceive their own coaching practice and their epistemological beliefs (Christian et al., 2017; Collins et al., 2015). Another study examined why individuals seek coaching in the context of adventure sports, which revealed that the clients emphasised three different but not mutually exclusive reasons to pursue coaching, in that their learning was: holistic, authentic, and developmental (Eastabrook & Collins, 2020). Gender is not considered a topic for exploration in these studies, and is only mentioned in the samples – which generally just consisted of men.

In Ellmer and Rynne's studies (2016, 2019), they focus on the concepts of both action sports and adventure sports, exemplified with their research into snowboarding, surfing, skateboarding, bicycle motor-cross (BMX), sports climbing and parkour. Their first publication (2016) examines the learning trajectory of an international-level Trials athlete – a woman. They describe how she took a strong role in her own learning while leveraging her peers and coach for learning opportunities at different stages of her career. The second study (2019) focuses on the professionalisation and organisation of action sports in the Australian context, based on a systematic literature review of both academic journals and 'grey literature' (i.e. magazines, websites, annual and research reports, government documents, etc.) (p. 1744). The sports in question were BMX, skateboarding, and surfing, all recently included in the Olympic Games. The findings revealed differences among the sports with regard to coach development and accreditation, athletes' development in terms of formal and informal learning, and the implications of new and social media technologies.

Skateboarding was also the focus of Jones' (2011) study. He examined the use of digital media in skateboarders' learning processes, in particular how the production and consumption of amateur videos contributed to the skaters' mastery of techniques as well as their integration into the skating culture. The participants in the study were all male skaters, as the author noted that female skaters were relatively rare, which was 'consistent with demographics of the sport worldwide' (p. 607).

Media of various kinds – mass media, niche media, and micro media – has played a vital role in snowboarding, specifically in regard of advertisement, self-promotion by the riders, and learning among novice as well as experienced snowboarders (Thorpe, 2008, 2011, 2012). Howe (1998) described the meaning of snowboarding media, how photographers and filmmakers commonly cooperated together with professional riders, and how their representations had a great influence on the snowboarding community. In this study, Howe sited Doug Palladini, publisher of the *Snowboarder* magazine: 'The magazines got so powerful because [of] the nature of our audience.' He continued: 'snowboarders are passionate consumers. For them, the magazines are not just something you pick up at the airport. To the core, it is the bible' (Howe, 1998, p. 104). In the earlier days of snowboarding, niche media – particularly videos and films – were vital channels for conveying snowboarding knowledge in a broad sense, and a source for the participants to learn new tricks – both in terms of how to perform them and the names of the tricks.

Coaching and learning in snowboarding

A few recent studies have discussed the role of the coach and learning strategies as well as more technical issues related to performance and skills enhancement. Ojala and Thorpe (2015) focused on the role of the coach while advocating for the use of a problem-based learning approach (PBL). Their approach is grounded in snowboarding's individualistic and anti-authoritarian traditions, for which peer-mentoring used to be a central element in an athlete's learning process. The study was based on observations and conversations with 28 freestyle snowboarders, including both women and men. A central issue uncovered here, was the unique value system in the sport that must be fore-grounded in any coach–athlete relationship, in addition to the value of the coaches' former experiences as elite snowboarders. Among the findings were perceived benefits among the learners of coaching in respect of one's skill level. In that regard, gender was mentioned in just one sentence: 'Both male and female participants suggested that coaches might only be valuable for lesser skilled riders such as up-and-coming athletes and female snowboarders' (p. 66). The issue was, however, not discussed further. In a comment relating to the article, Collins et al. (2016) questioned the PBL approach as '*the* answer' (p. 90) instead suggesting other approaches and arguing that also higher level/elite snowboarders might also benefit from coaching. However, none of the authors mentioned gender in their article either.

Two of the authors, Willmott and Collins went on to publish two more articles based on freeskiing and snowboarding. The first focuses on balancing the advancement of one's progress and minimising their injuries. Through a biopsychosocial perspective, they identified major factors that seem to influence both performance progression and the likelihood of sustaining an injury, while also taking the unique cultural and social milieu into account (Willmott & Collins, 2015). Gender issues are again not touched upon, except for one reference to a study on injuries in snowboarding where no differences between women and men were detected. The second article (Willmott & Collins, 2017) examines trick progression among elite freeskiers and snowboarders based on interviews with eight participants – three women and five men, from New Zealand and the United Kingdom all of whom represented their country at the Sochi 2014 Winter Olympics, with six of them achieving top ten results, while the two remaining athletes were injured. The results revealed that trick progression was achieved intermittently, moving through different stages during the year, and was subject to experiencing the right conditions, training facilities, competition periods and successful rehabilitation from injuries. Furthermore, the results covered time spent training on and off-snow, including different modalities such as the use of trampolines and airbags. Gender issues are not discussed here either, even though the quotes from athletes refer to them as numbers, based on their discipline, as freeskiing/snowboarding and whether they were female/male.

Following these two articles, Willmott (2019) wrote a chapter in the *Routledge Handbook of Elite Sport Performance* where he discusses methods for skill enhancement in snowboarding and freeskiing, with particular reference to 'park and pipe events', those of half-pipe, slopestyle and big air. With respect to skill enhancement, he suggests three developmental stages: the first relates to participants aged 5–10, then 10–14, and then the 14–18 age band. He includes reminders regarding the element of risk, in terms of technical requirements and the ever-changing environments due to snow conditions, weather, and particular challenges depending on the venue. It can be concluded from this then that he is particularly concerned with the athletes' preparation work, where trampolines have been a useful tool, and more recently the use of airbags which has made a significant difference in the progression of tricks and various manoeuvres. He elaborates on the methodology and relevant aspects in general terms, while also specifically referring to both coaches and athletes as she or he. For example, he notes that due to the innovatory dimension of the sport, there is 'the need for the coach to be developing moves that he or she may have never attempted' (p. 50).

Coaching female and male snowboarders

This section is mainly based on interviews conducted with the four coaches, divided into four parts. The first part gives an overview of the contexts the interviewed coaches worked within, for example, whether they are coaching young athletes at the start of their careers, or whether they are coaching athletes already competing at an elite level. The second relates to skill enhancement in how the coaches experienced handling female and male riders, specifically with regard to how to help them improve. The third focuses on communication in the coach – athlete relationship. In the last part, I will discuss the findings of research conducted based on coaching male and female athletes in general.

Context

I will start by contextualising the training athletes are provided, first at the secondary school and thereafter the national teams. The school is one of several secondary schools that operate under the title of Norges Toppidrettsgymnas (NTG), Norwegian Topsport High school in English. These schools assist school-aged athletes by combining sport with their secondary school education. The schools mainly focus on winter sports, and a few have included snowboarding in recent years. As these schools are located at winter sport destinations, the students have to move away from home (except for those who happen to grow up in the area), and they are housed in private lodgings. The schools operate as private schools that receive some financial support from the state. Thus, attending such a school requires considerable economic investment in terms of school fees, lodging, equipment and other costs related to attending camps and competitions, which means that this kind of education and career path is not open to everyone.

For the snowboarding pathway, the academic programme is adjusted depending on snowboarding practice and competitions. For their school curricula, female and male students are taught together, and this also applies for the snowboarding lessons. With respect to gender, males usually compose the majority of students, although this does vary from year to year. The former coach (female) noted that, on average, they could anticipate that female athletes would make up about one third of the annual cohort. The current coach (male) at the school had the figures from last year's cohort, which show that there were six female and ten male students. He emphasised that they actively work to recruit more females, including through collaboration with the snowboard federation.

The ski resort nearby the school provides excellent facilities for on-snow training, and they also visit other resorts nearby and spend a week in the early autumn at a glacier/ski resort in the Alps. Off-snow training takes place at the school and in a sports hall with trampolines. The students are expected to participate in the Norwegian Cup for snowboarding as well as other regional competitions. The most advanced riders also participate in World Roockie Tour, which is a snowboarding and freeskiing competition for athletes under 18, which is open 'to everybody who wants to become professional action sport rider' (https://www.worldrookietour.com). The current coach (male) estimated that more male participants compete in this contest than their female counterparts, which seems reasonable considering the gender bias among potential participants.

When it comes to the national teams, the gender ratio is more uneven. For the 2021–2022 season, the senior team consisted of one woman and seven men, and the recruit team had three women and six men. The share of females on the recruit team was however less uneven than it used to be, as there were commonly only one or two females. Both teams follow similar programmes during the year. After a break at the end of the competition season, it is time to prepare for the next, with a combination of off-snow and on-snow training. Off-snow training is devoted to working towards general physical improvements; endurance, strength, leaping power, motoric ability and tricks commonly performed on a trampoline. On-snow training is conducted on glaciers in Switzerland and/or Austria during the autumn before the competition season starts. The members of the team practice together, but still have individual training programmes adjusted for each athlete. Even though the athletes follow their own individual training programmes, issues regarding gender, and how the sport seems to prioritise the progression of male athletes, are obvious when the team practice together. This was explained by the senior coach in that the males push each other when it comes to both support and competition, whereas the only female in the group is commonly left on her own, albeit still with support and feedback from the coach. The female recruits are in a slightly better position as there are three on the team. However, they are still vulnerable if one (or two) happen to dropout for a period when injuries occur.

The senior coach is employed full-time in the role, while the recruit coach is only employed in a half-time position. Most of the senior athletes are full-time snowboarders, except for two who have a part-time job in order to make ends mate. Financially, there is a mix of support and income from the federation and the sponsors. In contrast to most other sports, the snowboarders are responsible themselves to a great extent for finding a sponsor, however they do also receive some assistance from the federation in regard to contracts and the like, when needed. When sponsor contracts are attained on an individual basis, qualities beyond athletic merits apparently have an impact. According to the senior coach, to be well-known in the milieu, having an extrovert personality and being perceived as a nice person all count. He emphasised the difficulties of this practice as such: 'It's really a tough trade, both for women and men. So many riders to select from, and they [sponsors] mainly just want those at the very top.' He further explained that some women can really benefit from sponsors within the snowboarding industry, in regard to receiving equipment, goggles, energy drinks, etc., and he also pointed out a distinction between them and the men in this respect as he said: 'It's probably a bit typical of women, that they manage to attract others (sponsors) to the sport, and then suddenly there's watches and that kind of thing that you don't tend to find in snowboarding.' Indeed, this may reflect the sponsor's choice of who to sponsor in considering their potential audience, in that they want to reach customers through the figure of a successful, sporty women.

The athletes' social media profiles also appear to be vital in whether or not sponsorship is a possibility, mainly if they post self-promoting posts, and they are active on social media, as the coach explained: 'Having loads of followers on Instagram and appreciating their fans and such, today that counts almost as much as being on the top of the podium.' This statement aligns with the research conducted by Thorpe and Dumont (2019), who described the importance of building one's audience via social media platforms, and thus gaining and maintaining sponsors based on their digital appearance and success when it comes to connecting with other consumer groups.

The recruit team is less professional than the seniors in terms of finance, time spent with the team, and performance level. Being employed part-time means that the coach's time with the team is limited and is mostly spent when at camps and other meetups. Beyond that, the snowboarders follow their individual programmes and practice on their own. The average age range on the team is between 18 and 22 years old. The participants are recruited from the secondary schools or by other riders representing their local clubs in national competitions, as the coach said: 'They are usually first recognised in the Norwegian Cup events. And, it's a small milieu so we know or recognise who's on the way up, so we hear rumors here and there, and of course we're around ourselves.'

Skill enhancement

In the discussions about skill enhancement, the findings revealed differences related to gender as well as performance level. One central theme relates to the athletes' agency in their own learning and skills development. The coaches at the secondary school and the coach for the recruit team all agreed that the male athletes appear more self-driven, which was explained in several ways. For example, in the context of school, the male students appeared to quickly get into the activities, whereas the female students were more often likely to wait to be told what to do. Integral to this then: the male students appear more proactive, tend to make more runs and repetitions, and generally make better use of the terrain and the variety of elements in the park, as the female coach explained:

> I realise that the girls are not that self-driven. This probably sounds like a bit of generalisation, but when the girls reach the top of the lift, they just do what they've been told, and then return to the lift. Whereas with the boys, on their way down to the park, they'll look for a side hit suitable for doing a backflip, then find another side hit to do a new trick, tend to play around more. And I think that comes from the social environment they grew up in, pushing each other from they were smaller, they're more likely to be like 'let's try this one', while the girls are more like, they'll just do the run, and if they do, they'll try to make a trick on a jump, but they get so focused on that particular trick, that after landing, they just pass by all other elements in the park. Somewhat overstated, but there is something in it.

To my follow-up question; why do boys tend to be more proactive than the girls in trying out the different elements, she suggested that female athletes may experience park-riding to be a bit intimidating, so they put so much energy into making a trick, so they don't have any more to try anything else, while also adding: 'I think the number of hours of quality on the board is reflected in board control.' The latter refers to her observation of male students spending more time snowboarding compared to their female counterparts. A similar observation was expressed by the other secondary school coach in that male students would spend more time snowboarding, and therefore showed faster rates of improvements, as he explained: 'I think it probably has a lot to do with movement experience.'

The senior national team coach revealed a different perspective; however, this was only based on two athletes, one who was part of the team, and another had recently quit. He mostly spoke of the latter, who had been on the team for longer. She was more experienced and ranked higher in terms of accomplishments. He described her as very determined, well-structured, with clear ideas about where to go, and what to emphasise during training, as he said: 'She very much did her own thing.' He exemplified this in describing her strength training in how she considered balancing between muscle weight and movement performance, as such: 'Because if you get very strong, then your legs get heavier to move around which then has an impact on the rotations and how to make the landing, and stuff like that.' The way he described her left an impression that gender is less of a focal point at the elite level compared to lower levels. As such, his statement aligns with the perceptions of snowboarding facilities as presented in Chapter 4, in which the elite, female snowboarders generally seemed to favour the use of the same facilities for both women and men in competitions.

Another central theme relates to the issue of risk, more precisely: how the coaches experience the athletes' behaviour in relation to risk. All of them agree that, generally, the male snowboarders are more open to risk-taking than the females. This was explained with the coaches' evaluation of conse-quences and self-confidence, as explained by the senior coach: 'The boys love to take chances, and such, have a bigger ego than many of the girls. They are full of themselves and have confidence in their own skills.' The interviewees explained in various ways that the female athletes are more reflexive in their thinking when it comes to the consequences of their actions, as the male sec-ondary school coach said: 'The girls reflect quite a lot, for good and bad, and the boys probably a bit less.' The expression 'for good and bad' indicating here both positive as well as negative effects, which he further explained as:

> The boys probably don't always think through the things they do, and that may result in good riding, good tricks and a lot of excitement, whereas the girls often think through what they are doing well, and that's fine when talking about making the right choices, but it maybe also hinders them from developing at the same rate as the boys.

The final sentence here refers to developing snowboarding skills, which ap-parently relates to the athlete's level of self-confidence, something confirmed through the statements of all four coaches. The senior coach said of this: 'My experience is that the girls, more than the boys, are doubtful about their per-formance when there are risks involved' which was mentioned in regard to speed and riding conditions. The recruit team coach was particularly con-cerned about ensuring that the female athletes felt confident in their efforts towards progressing tricks. He commonly rode together with them, or before them on the jumps to 'show, so they feel safe, that they're not alone in doing it, that we are two.' He further explained the necessity of teaching such things in a step-by-step approach with the various elements composing the overall, final, trick, to keep them feeling safe. Apparently, a central issue in this regard is keeping them motivated to try more and step outside of their comfort zone. In some cases, he explained, that the riders set a new trick in a competition for the first time. Similar stories came from the coaches at the secondary school, which really surprised me. In my thinking, it would be more logical if the fe-male riders repeatedly made the tricks before a competition, so as to feel safe, but this actually seemed to be the opposite. It should be added, however, that Stine Brun Kjeldaas (former elite snowboarder) also noted that she often only made a new trick for the first time, in a competition, because:

> It's like that with the McTwist (front flip combined with the 540 rota-tion), and other flips and things like that, I thought it was horrifying. But

I had to in order to keep up, but I wouldn't dare to do it during practice. Almost never tried it when training, so in competitions I just had to, the only chance I had was in the competitions, otherwise I wouldn't be able to make myself do it.

I found her story quite interesting and went on to ask how she prepared for the tricks, to which she answered that she practiced on the trampoline, and 'visualised it a thousand times, so I know what to do.' In comparison, Willmott and Collins (2017) reported from their study of elite snowboarders that a number of their participants had only landed a trick for the first time during a competition, after having prepared on the trampoline and/or airbag, and that this visualisation therefore appeared to be of vital importance.

The third theme relates to bodily reactions when unforeseen/challenging situations occur, which are first and foremost connected to the jumps and aerial movements. The coaches agreed that the female snowboarders found such situations more difficult to manage. The senior coach explained:

With the girls, if anything goes wrong while in the air, they tend to get stiff, and sort of freeze and just follow the set run, that axis. If you start rushing forward, for example, during the trick, and get off the jump on the wrong line, then it's easy to fall flat on your face. I've seen it many times in competitions, whereas the guys, for example, quickly search for a way out, they may realise early like 'oh shit, I am not going fast enough' when they reach the jump, and that the take-off may be wrong. The guys are more aware. I don't really know how to explain, but they sort of, when something goes wrong, they behave like cats, so they land on their feet, in the best possible manner, to avoid being injured.

It is interesting here to note the expression 'behave like cats', as this also aligns again with Willmott and Collins's study (2017), where they examined factors that promote progression, and different training modalities in elite snowboarding, including on-snow versus off-snow practice. One such aspect that was particularly emphasised was physicality and robustness training (strength, power, and endurance), namely the use of trampolines where an ability for cat-like fitness – meaning always landing on your feet – was promoted. This kind of ability was perceived to be important both in regard to injury prevention and a performance enhancement perspective. The study did not mention gender in relation to the athletes' abilities. However, when considering the findings of that study and the coach's statement referred above, it seems reasonable to suggest that in elite snowboarding male athletes are perceived as being much further ahead than the female athletes, and the standard in evaluations of skills enhancement as well as the ability to manage difficult situations.

The secondary school coaches revealed comparable perceptions of female riders when they lose control and struggle to manage the situation. The female coach gave one example of such a reaction, explaining that some girls tend to close their eyes. When I asked whether that happened to girls only, not to boys, she said 'maybe, but I haven't heard of it, but the girls do it.' I wondered if closing their eyes meant they then tried to visualise the trick, to which she answered: 'No, you get scared. Because, if you make a mistake and feel like, now this is it [it's going wrong], and just, yes, I think it's on reflex.' The male coach repeated his perception of movement experience as mentioned above while explaining that: 'A lot of it's about having been in a similar situation before, that you react based on experience. Yes, maybe, don't get a chance to think, you just do it on impulse, or of instinct.' This statement circles back to what we understand as *tacit knowledge* which reflects one's unconscious, embodied agency, as explained by Polyani and Prosch (1975) as when 'these feelings are not watched *in themselves* but that I watch something else by keeping aware of them' (p. 33). Hence, the tacit knowledge may appear when the movements of a trained athlete seem, to a large extent, to be automatic, and which appear to be the result of long-term focused practice. Yet, it's interesting to note the senior coach's observation of gender-specific behaviour, when discussing elite snowboarders, which should supposedly be automatic and natural in terms of these repeated movements.

Communication in the athlete–coach relationship

The coaches' descriptions of communication between themselves and the athletes varied according to the performance level and group composition. The secondary school coaches discussed this in regard to both males and females in the context of school, as well as their general impression they've picked up over their years of working in the field. The national team coaches referred primarily to their teams, for which the athletes have more individually focused programmes and received individual feedback and support.

Some of their perception of communication mirrored the themes discussed in the former section on skills enhancement. For example, the observation of male athletes as more self-driven is reflected in their styles of communication too, namely in the way that female athletes are more receptive to feedback, and they need more follow-up support, which appears important for them in terms of helping to create that feeling of security. This is particularly the case when there are few women in the group, as the recruit coach explained: 'When we have practice together, the girls are often overshadowed by the boys, the boys take up far more space. So, we must push the boys away a bit and check in more with the girls.' Similarly, the male secondary school coach explained that the female athletes needed more affirmation, whereas 'with some of the boys, it's more like it's their project, they don't want others to get too involved.'

Another aspect of communication relates to the coaches' way of speaking, where a common understanding seemed to be that they could be more direct when addressing the male athletes compared to the female athletes. The female coach was quite clear on this when I asked whether she takes a different approach when it comes to coaching female and male students, to which she answered with a laugh 'Yes, for certain' while adding: 'there we have missed badly all of us.' She further explained the necessity of being cautious with the females, particularly in dialogue relating to their tricks' development:

> You must not be seen as pushy, for example when suggesting how to proceed with a trick, what's the next step, especially when they find it a bit scary, and if they can't bring themselves to say anything about it, then that's when they get a bit discouraged.

The male secondary school coach and the recruit team coach revealed similar perceptions, for example what kind of encouragement you can give the riders at the top of the slope, before a run, which seems to have a greater impact on a female rider compared to a male, which again relates to self-confidence and being self-driven in situations where they can make progress.

Yet another aspect in the findings related to power dynamics during practice, where the research indicates that more negotiation is required in the female athlete–coach relationship than in the male athlete–coach relationship. The secondary school coaches and the recruit coach explained how they were open to the female athletes' suggestions of doing things, in terms of things such as 'how they wanted to get the feedback' and 'how they wanted to be pushed', whereas the males could just be told 'do this or that' and then they did. When the coach did some filming of the athletes, the males would just watch this on their own while the females needed to watch along with the coach and discuss the performance. The senior team coach related his experiences of the two athletes on the team, and mostly referred to the former, who would apparently take the lead in such discussions. After a run, for example, he used to ask for her view, before he commented:

> When I approached her, she wouldn't me to tell her anything, she wanted to tell me, and then I just had to agree or maybe disagree a bit, but mostly I agreed and probably suggest how to moderate it a bit. So, it was mostly about supporting her.

This statement indicates that there was a balanced relationship of power here, where the athlete took the lead in discussing her performance and progression, which may reflect her level of accomplishment, as well as her own development into the elite level as a very determined athlete, as already noted. When considering all these aspects combined, the coaches' stories seem to indicate more even power relations in snowboarding than in 'traditional' competitive sports, which also supports the proposal put forward by Ojala and Thorpe (2015), who argue for the use of a PBL approach, where coaches should help the athletes in finding the right answer, and support them in 'finding their own solution to a situation in which they may be experiencing difficulties' (p. 68).

How do the findings correspond with former research?

The findings presented above can be categorised into three main themes. First, that male athletes are perceived as more self-driven than female athletes. This may be connected to the male-dominated field in which they perform, where male athletes take up more space and see themselves as superior to their female counterparts – or behave as such more or less unconsciously (Anderson, 1999; Pettersson & Wennberg-Olsson, 2015). The latter commonly results in women's withdrawal from various snowboarding contexts, as revealed in my own research (Sisjord, 2009, 2013).

The second theme concerns risk-taking, where the overall impression is that male snowboarders are more comfortable taking risks than female snowboarders. This assumption reflects much of the existing research on risk-taking and extreme/risk sport, where risk-taking commonly is associated with masculinity and male-dominated contexts (Atencio et al., 2009; Laurendeau, 2008; V. Robinson 2004, 2010; Stranger, 2007). The picture is, however, not clear cut, as many female snowboarders have also internalised the cultural value system in the sport and celebrate courage and risk-taking, while experiencing their share of injuries (Thorpe, 2007, 2011, 2012). Furthermore, an increase in women's participation in risk-taking activities demonstrates that women are in fact, also attracted to the same thrill-seeking experiences as their male counterparts (Stranger, 2007).

The third theme revolves around communication within the coach–athlete relationship, which is reflected in the way coaches approach the athletes. In general, female athletes appeared to be more receptive to and dependent on feedback, support and encouragement from the coach, which was explained in terms of a lack of self-confidence and belief in their own abilities. These observations correspond with the former research, which describes female athletes as more coachable, while also being more sensitive to criticism and more prone to struggling with their confidence (Janssen, 2013), and additionally that female athletes tend to put more emphasis on positive communication, to feel comfortable and respected in the coach–athlete relationship (Gilbert, 2016; LaVoi, 2007; Norman, 2015). Studies have also revealed that perceptions of gender differences impact the coaches' style of communication. Female coaches as well as male coaches seem to speak more directly and in a tougher manner to male athletes than to the female athletes (MacKinnon, 2011; Sisjord et al., 2019.

Focusing on gender differences in coaching is, however, a double-edged issue. On one side, acquiring knowledge about the athletes' desires and behaviours is essential to be able to accommodate for the most favourable practice. On the other hand, one should be cautious not to stereotype athletes according to gender categories and in turn, disregard the diversity of the athletes' needs – both males and females. Integral to this, one should be aware of the gendered sport contexts: how coaches are socialised in masculine discourses, during practice as well as in coach education, as exemplified by Avner et al.'s (2019) study. In this study, they examined how coaches and athletes understand 'fun' differently when it comes to physical skills training. Although 'fun' is a term that lacks conceptual clarity, it appeared to be used as a strategy to naturalise various sporting practices. Among the findings was the fact that the coaches perceived that the female athletes held a stronger emphasis on social bonding, whereas the male athletes were more focused on demonstrating their mental toughness and masculinity. Theoretically, the study was informed by Foucault, and one of the conclusions made was that the incorporation of fun further legitimised and perpetuated the coaches' training practices. Also inspired by Foucault, Jones et al. (2020) discussed 'gender effective coaching' based on a fictive case of a coaching/competition situation in a women's team, for which the coach kept gender-specific considerations in mind when interacting and communicating with the team after a match, where one of the players felt bad about her accomplishment. Simply put: the implications of the study were that coaching knowledge and practices must be considered as fluid, and as such open to change.

References

Acosta, V. & Carpenter, L.J. (2014). *Women in Intercollegiate Sport. A Longitudinal National Study Thirty-Seven Year Update, 1977–2014.* Brooklyn College. DOI:10.1123/wspaj.9.2.141

Alsarve, D. (2018). Addressing gender equality: Enactments of gender and hegemony in the educational textbooks used in Swedish sports coaching and educational programmes. *Sport, Education and Society, 23*(9), 840–852. DOI:10.1080/13573322.2017.1280012

Anderson, K. (1999). Snowboarding. The construction of gender in an emerging sport. *Journal of Sport and Social Issues, 23*(1), 55–79.

Atencio, M., Beal, B. & Wilson, C. (2009). The distinction of risk: Urban skateboarding, street habitus and the construction of hierarchical gender relations. *Qualitative Research in Sport and Exercise, 1*(1), 3–20. DOI:10.1080/19398440802567907

Avner, Z., Denison, J. & Markula, P. (2019). 'Good athletes have fun': A Foucauldian reading of university coaches' uses of fun. *Sports Coaching Review, 8*(1), 43–61.

Christian, E., Berry, M. & Kearney, P. (2017). The identity, epistemology and developmental experiences of high-level adventure sports coaches. *Journal of Adventure Education and Outdoor Learning, 17*(4), 353–366. DOI:10.1080/14729679.2017.1341326

Collins, D.J., Collins, L. & Willmott, T. (2016). Over egging the pudding? Comments on Ojala and Thorpe. *International Sport Coaching Journal, 3*, 90–93. DOI:10.1123/iscj.2015-0068

Collins, L. & Collins, D. (2012). Conceptualizing the adventure-sports coach. *Journal of Adventure Education & Outdoor Learning, 12*(1), 81–93.

Collins, L. & Collins, D. (2013). Decision making and risk management in adventure sports coaching. *Quest, 65*, 72–82. DOI:10.1080/14729679.2014.950592

Collins, L., Collins, D. & Grecic, D. (2015). The epistemological chain in high-level adventure sports coaches. *Journal of Adventure Education and Outdoor Learning, 15*(3), 224–238. DOI:10.1080/14729679.2014.950592

Demers, G. (2009) "We are coaches": Program tackles the under-representation of female coaches. *Canadian Journal for Women in Coaching*, 9(2). http://23361.vws. magma.ca/WOMEN/e/journal/april2009/index.htm

Eastabrook, C. & Collins, L. (2020). Why do individuals seek out adventure sport coaching? *Journal of Adventure Education and Outdoor Learning*, 20(3), 245–258. DOI:10.1080/14729679.2019.1660192

Ellmer, E. & Rynne, S. (2016). Learning in action and adventure sports. *Asia-Pacific Journal of Health, Sport and Physical Education*, 7(2), 107–119. DOI:10.1080/ 18377122.2016.1196111

Ellmer, E. & Rynne, S. (2019). Professionalisation of action sports in Australia. *Sport in Society*, 22(10), 1742–1757. DOI:10.1080/17430437.2018.1440700

Etnier, J.L. (2011). Considerations in coaching girls and women in sport and physical activity settings. *Women in Sport and Physical Activity Journal*, 20(1), 98–100.

Fasting, K., Sisjord, M.K. & Sand, T.S. (2017). Norwegian elite-level coaches: Who are they? *Scandinavian Sport Studies Forum ISSN 20000-088X*, 8, 29–47.

Gathercole, R.J., Stellingwerff, T. & Sporer, B.C. (2015). Effect of acute fatigue and training adaptation on countermovement jump performance in elite snowboard cross athletes. *Journal of Strength and Conditioning Research*, 29(1), 37–46.

Gilbert, W. (2016). Coaching males/coaching females. Human kinetics: Coach education center. http://www.asep.com/news/ShowArticle.cfm?ID=260

Grahn, K. (2014). Youth athletes, bodies and gender: Gender constructions in textbooks used in coaching education programmes in Sweden. *Sport, Education and Society*, 19(6), 735–751. DOI:10.1080/13573322.2012.722549

Gray, P. & Collins, D. (2016). The adventure sports coach: All show and no substance? *Journal of Adventure Education and Outdoor Learning*, 16(2), 160–171.

Hovden, J. & Tjønndal, A. (2019). The gendering of coaching from an athletic perspective: The case of Norwegian boxing. *International Review for the Sociology of Sport*, 54(2), 239–255. DOI:10.1177/1012690217715641

Howe, S. (1998). *(Sick) a Cultural History of Snowboarding*. St Martin's Press.

Janssen, J. (2013). *Special Report: Discover the 8 Differences Between Men and Women – Part 1*. Championship Coaches Network. http:www.championshipcoachesnetwork. com/public/375.cfm

Jeon, Y. & Eom, K. (2021). Role of physique and fitness in the balance of Korean national snowboard athletes. *Journal of Exercise Science & Fitness*, 19, 1–7. DOI:10.1016/j.jesf.2020.07.001

Jones, L., Mills, J. & Avner, Z. (2020). Learning to problematise 'the way things are' when coaching female athletes. In Cope, E. & Partington, M. (Eds.), *Sports Coaching. A Theoretical and Practical Guide* (pp. 135–145). Routledge.

Jones, R.H. (2011). Sport and re/creation: What skateboarders can teach us about learning. *Sport, Education and Society*, 16(5), 593–611. DOI:10.1080/13573322.2011. 601139

Laurendeau, J. (2008). 'Gendered risk regimes': A theoretical consideration of edgework and gender. *Sociology of Sport Journal*, 25, 239–886.

LaVoi, N.M. (2007). Expanding the interpersonal dimension: Closeness in the coach-athlete relationship. *International Journal of Sports Science & Coaching*, 2(4), 497–512.

LaVoi, N.M., Becker, E. & Maxwell, H.D. (2007). "Coaching girls": A content analysis of best-selling popular press coaching books. *Women in Sport and Physical Activity Journal*, 15(4), 7–20.

MacKinnon, V. (2011). Techniques for instructing female athletes in traditionally male sports: A case study of LPGA teaching professionals. *The International Journal of Sport and Society, 2*(1), 77–87. DOI:10.18848/2152-7857/CGP/v02i01/54060

Norman, L. (2015). The coaching needs of high performance female athletes within the coach-athlete dyad. *International Sport Coaching Journal, 2*, 15–28.

Norman, L. (2016). Is there a need for coaches to be more gender responsive? A review of the evidence. *International Sport Coaching Journal, 3*, 192–196.

Norman, L. & French, J. (2013). Understanding how high performance women athletes experience the coach-athlete relationship. *International Journal of Coaching Science, 7*(1), 3–24.

Ojala, A-L. & Thorpe, H. (2015). The role of the coach in action sports: Using a problem-based learning approach. *International Sport Coaching Journal, 2*(1), 64–71. DOI:10.1123/iscj.2014-0096

Pettersson, J.H. & Wennberg-Olsson, L. (2015). 'Killar kommer alltid vara bättre, så är livet att vara tjei': En kvalitativ undersökning om kvinnors plats inom sporterna snowboard och freeskiing. ['The guys will always do better', that's life as a girl': A qualitative study about women's place in the sports of snowboarding and freeskiing] Idrottsvetenskapliga programmet, Pedagogiska institutionen. [The Sport Science Programme. Institute of Education.] University of Umeå.

Pfister, G. (2013). Outsiders: Female coaches intruding upon a male domain. In Pfister, G. & Sisjord, M.K. (Eds.), *Gender and Sport. Changes and Challenges* (pp. 71–99). Waxmann.

Platzer, H.-P., Raschner, C., Patterson, C. & Lembert, S. (2009). Comparison of physical characteristicsand performance among elite snowboarders. *Journal of Strength and Conditioning Research, 23*(5), 1427–1431. DOI:10.1519/JSC.0b013e3181aa1d9f

Polyani, M. & Prosch, H. (1975). *Meaning.* The University of Chicago Press.

Robertson, S. (2016). Hear their voices: Suggestions for developing and supporting women coaches from around the world. In LaVoi, N.M. (Ed.), *Women in Sports Coaching* (pp. 177–222). Routledge.

Robinson, P.E. (2010). *Foundations of Sports Coaching.* Routledge and Taylor & Francis Group.

Robinson, V. (2004). Taking risks: Identity, masculinities and rock climbing. In Wheaton, B. (Ed.), *Understanding Lifestyle Sports: Consumption, Identity and Difference* (pp. 113–130). Routledge.

Robinson, V. (2010). Researching everyday sporting masculinities: Thoughts from a (critical) distance. *Journal of Gender Studies, 19*(3) 309–313. DOI:10.1080/09589236.2010.494347

Sisjord, M.K. (2009). Fast-girls, babes and the invisible girls. Gender relations in snowboarding. *Sport in Society, 12*(10), 1299–1316. DOI:10.1080/17430430903204801

Sisjord, M.K. (2013). Women's snowboarding. Some experiences and perceptions of competitions. *Leisure Studies, 32*(5), 507–523. DOI:10.1080/02614367.2012.685334

Sisjord, M.K., Fasting, K. & Sand, T. T. (2019). *Elite Coaches' Perceptions of Coaching Female and Male Athletes.* Paper presented at the European Association for Sociology of Sport's conference, Bø in Telemark, June 3–6.

Sisjord, M.K., Fasting, K. & Sand, T.S. (2021). Gendered pathways to elite coaching reflecting the accumulation of capitals. *Sport, Education and Society, 26*(5), 554–566, DOI:10.1080/13573322.2020.1732904

Smith, E., Larson, A. & DeBeliso, M. (2015). The physical profile of elite boarder-cross snowboarders. *Journal of Sports Science, 3*, 272–281. DOI:10.17265/2332-7839/2015.06.002

Staniszewski, M., Zybko, P. & Wiszomirska, I. (2016). Evaluation of laterality in the snowboard basic position. *Human Movement, 17*(2), 119–125. DOI:10.1515/humo-2016-0015

Stranger, M. (2007). Sociology of risk. In Booth, D. & Thorpe, H. (Eds.), *Berkshire Encyclopedia of Extreme Sports* (pp. 294–302). Berkshire Publishing Group.

Thorpe, H. (2007). Snowboarding. In Thorpe, H. & Booth, D. (Eds.), *Berkshire Encyclopedia of Extreme Sports* (pp. 286–294). Berkshire Publishing.

Thorpe, H. (2008). Foucault, technologies of self, and the media. Discourses of femininity in snowboarding culture. *Journal of Sport & Social Issues, 32*(2), 199–229. DOI:10.1177/0193723508315206

Thorpe, H. (2011). *Snowboarding Bodies in Theory and Practice*. Palgrave Macmillan.

Thorpe, H. (2012). *Snowboarding: The Ultimate Guide*. Greenwood Press.

Thorpe, H. & Dumont, G. (2019). The professionalization of action sports: Mapping trends and future directions. *Sport in Society, 22*(10), 1639–1654.

Turnbull, J., Keogh, J.W.L. & Kilding, A.E. (2011). Strength and conditioning considerations for elite snowboard half pipe. *The Open Sports Medicine Journal, 5*, 1–11. DOI:10.2174/1874387001105010001

Vernillo, G., Pisoni, C. & Thiebat, G. (2016a). Physiological characteristics of elite snowboarders. *Journal of Sports Medicine and Physical Fitness, 56*(5), 527–533.

Vernillo, G., Pisoni, C. & Thiebat, G. (2016b). Strength asymmetry between front and rear leg in elite snowboard athletes. *Clinical Journal of Sport Medicine, 26*(1), 83–85.

Vernillo, G., Pisoni, C., Sconfienza, L.M., Thiébat, G. & Longo, S. (2017). Changes in muscle architecture of vastus lateralis muscle after an alpine snowboarding race. *Journal of Strenght and Conditioning Research, 31*(1), 254–259. DOI:10.1519/JSC.0000000000001469

Vernillo, G., Pisoni, C. & Thiébat, G. (2018). Physiological and physical profile of snowboarding: A preliminary review. *Frontiers in Physiology*, published 20. June 1–7. DOI:10.3389/fphys.2018.00770

Willmott, T. (2019). Coaching in action/adventure sports – A novel challenge. In Collins, D., Cruickshank, A. & Jordet, G. (Eds.), *Routledge Handbook of Elite Sport Performance* (pp. 47–57). Routledge and Taylor & Francis Group.

Willmott, T. & Collins, D. (2015). Challenges in the transition to mainstream: Promoting progress and minimizing injury in freeskiing and snowboarding. *Sport in Society, 18*(10), 1245–1259.

Willmott, T. & Collins, D. (2017). A retrospective analysis of trick progression in elite freeskiing and snowboarding. *International Sport Coaching Journal, 4*(1), 1–12.

Zebrowska, A., Zyta, D., Kania, D. & Langfort, J. (2012). Anaerobic and aerobic performance of elite female and male snowboarders. *Journal of Human Kinetics, 34*, 81–88. Section II- Exercise Physiology & Sports Medicine. DOI:10.2478/v10078-012-0066-9

6 Female snowboarders in various contexts

From the early days of snowboarding, male snowboarders have instilled in the sport a fearless, aggressive and masculine style, which has gone on to influence the wider snowboarding culture and gender relations within the sport, as has been explored in several studies (e.g. Anderson, 1999; Thorpe, 2004). A central aspect of this research is that of the position of women in snowboarding; that is whether they are proactive or passive in their participation, and whether they are perceived by the wider community as being one or the other. Women who demonstrate courage and sporting prowess may gain status in the snowboarding culture. Passive women, commonly conforming to traditional gender roles, may be labelled as *babes* or a *pro ho* (snowboarding's equivalent of groupies and the least respected group in the snowboarding environment) or even *poseurs* or *pretenders*, which is also a term that can be used for male riders who aren't respected by the inner core of snowboarders (Sisjord, 2009; Thorpe, 2005, 2009, 2011, 2012).

The two positions – proactive women who demonstrate courage and dedication versus those who take more passive roles in the sport – may be perceived as extreme opposites of the same spectrum: that of a gendered snowboarding culture. In between the two, there are many different categories, which applies to both genders; from occasional riders and weekend warriors to professional athletes. In the following chapter, I will present relevant research in the field to highlight the perception of women snowboarders in various snowboarding contexts, mainly based on the work of Holly Thorpe – who has published a significant number of publications within the field of snowboarding – as well as my own studies. I will then consider two of the themes extracted from the interviews carried out for the purpose of this book. The first relates to the secondary school coaches and their experiences in teaching both female and male students, in terms of helping them to develop snowboarding skills and their possible trajectory into elite snowboarding. The second relates to the experiences of the WSF president during her time spent in the top positions of international snowboarding.

DOI: 10.4324/9781003007098-6

Previous research

In one of her earlier works, Thorpe (2005) examined women's positions and opportunities in snowboarding, mainly in reference to professional snowboarders. By adopting a historical sociological approach, she explored the construction, renegotiation and possible reconstruction of gender relations in snowboarding contexts. Her analysis covered topics such as role models, camaraderie versus increasing individualism, women in the snowboarding industry, and equal versus limited opportunities. She painted contrasting pictures of the female snowboarders, one more optimistic, indicating the existence of social progress, and the other more negative, highlighting the issues of social constraints. She discussed the two scenarios in light of which approach to feminism may benefit the sport, specifically looking at liberal feminism and radical feminism, in which she concluded that liberal feminism has a greater potential to enact change when it comes to altering gender relations. While the existing social structure within snowboarding does continue to privilege male snowboarders, she argued that growing levels of participation and opportunities brought about by an increase in female-focused initiatives may support the development of strong, individual women, unafraid to challenge their male counterparts.

In one of her later publications, Thorpe (2009) builds on Bourdieu's conceptualisation, explaining how certain forms of femininity, preferred forms of capital (cultural, social and symbolic) and gender relations differ between various groups within the field of snowboarding. She examined how female snowboarders either benefit from or lose symbolic capital in different ways depending on their investment in cultural capital, which can be defined in terms of their snowboarding knowledge and performance. The main issue is that in the male-defined symbolic structure of snowboarding, whatever form of capital females possess in one respect, they tend to lose in another. For example, women who choose to emphasise their feminine capital are often perceived as uncommitted to the activity and are written off as 'snow bunnies' (p. 495). On the other hand, women who possess masculine capital (typified as physical prowess, risk-taking and strong commitment) and who position themselves in opposition to the culturally valued discourse of stereotypical femininity, may consequently experience ideological constraints, and are even referred to as 'butch lesbians' regardless of their sexuality or how they identify (p. 495). However, Thorpe indicates that female snowboarders who hold a high position in the sport and who have valued capital in the field are seemingly able to overcome this quandary by actively blurring the boundaries that divide the two.

The categorisation of female snowboarders into different groups – such as the core snowboarders, weekend warriors and poseurs – also adds another dimension the women have to consider when blurring these lines. Of these categories, social class is also included, as class and gender are always intimately connected. Indeed, Laurendeau and Sharara (2008) recognise social class in their analysis of women in snowboarding and skydiving. They investigated the different ways that women who participate in these activities were limited, and the strategies they employed to overcome these and carve out spaces for themselves. In snowboarding, the women often felt that they were not taken seriously by the male riders, they felt uncomfortable and inadequate in certain areas – especially those that require advanced snowboarding skills and style, for example in the terrain parks. Many men and even some women explained that the lower participation rate among women in the sport is a product of women's unwillingness to take risks compared to that of the men.

In response to this, Laurendeau and Sharara's findings indicate that in both sports, women tend to employ strategies rooted in the middle-class and liberal notions of resistance, that reflect reproductive agency as well as resistance agency. Reproductive agency refers to women's behaviour when it contributes to maintaining unequal power relations, for example, when women tend to withdraw in the terrain park if the space is dominated by male riders, or when they underplay their physical abilities in other ways. Resistance agency was identified as situations in which female boarders engage in practices that aim to challenge the stereotype that women are less skilled than their male counterparts. However, their findings mostly refer to individual strategies the female snowboarders employ, of which the authors compiled to form their conclusion as to what collective strategies they believe these athletes could adopt going forward that could promote further resistance.

Gender inequality and the negotiation of female snowboarders for a space in within various snowboarding contexts were also themes explored in a study by Russell and Lemon (2012). The objective of their study was to explore the ways in which gendered performances are negotiated through the practice of 'jibbing' – which can be understood as performing 'diverse tricks on features usually found in a terrain park, such as boxes and rails' (p. 241). The study was conducted at a snowboarding and skiing location in Australia, based on semi-structured interviews with male and female snowboarders, aged 18–26, who were all experienced jibbers. The study takes a post-structural position, for which the authors adopted Butler's notion of gender performativity. The findings revealed that all of the interviewees agreed that male snowboarders dominate in the jobbing community. Not only were females in the minority, they were also perceived as less skilled. The female snowboarders in this field were generally viewed as one of two things – either '(a) as having "potential" if guided appropriately, or (b) as "at risk" physically' (p. 244). Yet, the male snowboarders were nonetheless explicit in their acceptance of women participating. The findings suggest that male participants often employ paternalistic ways of regulating female participation, and thereby reinforcing their male dominance in jibbing contexts.

Spowart et al. also based their research on post-structuralist theory, when studying snowboarding and motherhood, where they draw on Foucault's theoretical perspectives and concepts. For one such study (2008) they investigated the ways in which snowboarding mothers ensured that they could continue snowboarding after having a baby or while raising small children. The study explored how the women shape their own identities and social relations, resisting the social expectations created by the ideology of motherhood. The findings not only illustrate enjoyment and empowerment but also a feeling of guilt in taking time to themselves away from the family. However, it is also worth noting that, the women shared an enthusiasm for snowboarding with their spouse, they had support from other family members, and their jobs indicated that they belonged to a middle-class background. In a separate study, Spowart and Burrows (2016) focused on voluntary risk-taking in relation to discourses of care and motherhood. The interviewees had continued snowboarding during pregnancy and as a result, experienced various reactions to this from the people around them, which were mostly negative in terms of seeing the mothers as irresponsibile. However, in their own view, the women had been careful and controlled possible risk elements, but the findings did go on to reveal that the interviewees had become far more cautious since becoming parents.

In regard of my own studies, these mainly relate to the Norwegian context. Two of the studies were mentioned in the former chapter in light of discussions around snowboarding facilities. The first of which (Sisjord, 2009) was conducted in connection with a workshop organised by the Norwegian Snowboard Federation (NSBF) with the aim of discussing strategies for promoting women's snowboarding. The theoretical basis of this study draws on perspectives around subculture and Bourdieu's conceptualisation of field, capital, and masculine domination. This study resulted in a wide range of interesting views and findings, with two specific themes worthy of note in this particular context.

The first of these themes revolved around the interviewees' perceptions of different types of femininities among snowboarders, with the female snowboarders being divided into three groups: *babes*, *fast girls* and *the invisible girls*. These labels emerged from some of the interviewees' own descriptions, both of themselves and of others; for example, *babes* was a common term used in the snowboarding jargon, whereas *fast girls* appeared more self-identifying, and was generally used to describe how some participants viewed themselves and other pro-active women in the snowboarding community. The former term, *babes,* can be understood as female snowboarders who visit resorts, but mostly to meet male snowboarders and party, whereas the latter, *fast girls,* are understood as female snowboarders who strive to show their skills and challenge the hegemonic position of men. The third descriptor, *invisible girls,* was used to describe the silent group of female snowboarders who take to the slopes, and who are probably the greatest in number in the sport, but are the least visible. *Invisible girls* commonly withdraw in mixed gender contexts and were thus the most important target group for the organisers of the workshop.

The second theme reflects the overall impression extracted from the discussions among the participants, that female snowboarders – as a category – are perceived as 'second-class snowboarders' (p. 1305) especially when it comes to snowboarding competitions. The interviewees were unhappy about the minor interest shown to female snowboarders by the speakers at competitions, namely those who introduce the riders and provide commentary on their performance, primarily those of local and national contests. The speakers (always men) commonly provided fewer comments when the female riders were introduced and competed, in comparison to the male riders. A few even mentioned that the speaker neglected them entirely or would utter disrespectful comments. One of the interviewees said: 'It's no fun when the speaker is more focused on how your trousers fit you, than on your tricks' (p. 1306). Other interviewees noted that some of the competitions for women were often held after the males' final had finished, or that the prizes for their competitions would be men's snowboarding boots or T-shirts, meaning they were always too big. Given the fact that Thorpe's (2005) study notes that equal opportunities and amount awarded in prize money and sponsorship can be considered as a sign of respect and status for female snowboarders, this lack of funding and consideration as to what the female snowboarders receive for winning such competitions is evidence of a continual imbalance. Together then, these studies thus brought to light the general inequality in the amount of prize money, the fact that competitions are designed for men, and other evidence of the devaluation and marginalisation of women in the sport.

The second study was conducted at the International Women's Snowboard Camp. This study (Sisjord, 2013) also made use of Bourdieu's theoretical framework, and similar to the first, one theme that emerged from the research was that of the status of women's participation in snowboarding competitions. The findings revealed various perceptions of competitions, reflecting the different performance levels among the interviewees, as well as past experiences. The most positive voice was one who had aspired to a professional career and participated in several international contests. However, due to injuries, combined with the uncertainty of making snowboarding their livelihood, she instead prioritised her education. She recalled that competitions were challenging, but added that she liked to test herself against others and to achieve the best of her ability. Another participant in the study had taken part in competitions at both the national and international levels, but described her participation in competitions as 'just a side-thing' (p. 513). This was because she was frequently in charge of organising contests instead, and visited events in order to see friends, get new ideas, and to compare said event with others. The other interviewees had less experience with competitions, which was attributed to either a lack of interest and/or not being skilled enough to enter. A couple of them expressed discomfort with competitions in terms of the mental strain it put on them. Apparently, this feeling of stress was mainly associated with the athletic performance required of them in jumps, where creativity and physical ability are essential elements of the participants' physical and symbolic capital.

The third of my publications to note here focused on the networking and relationships of female snowboarders with national snowboard associations and commercial organisers (Sisjord, 2012). The theoretical approaches employed included Castells' network theory and identity construction in social movements, combined with gender perspectives which first and foremost related to the concepts of doing/undoing gender. I solely refer to the findings that focused on the camp attendees' organisational relationships and level of agency in their home countries. The participants from the Nordic countries – Finland, Norway and Sweden – appeared more proactive in terms of defining their place and role in the organisational landscape, compared to the representatives from Italy and Latvia. The Finnish women had founded the Finnish Female Snowboarding Association (FFSA), a small association in terms of the number of members, but influential in terms of their motivation and innovation. The leader of the FFSA explained how the association came about:

> In the beginning, we felt like nobody was doing anything for girls, so it was kind of our idea that we did not want, things were a bit, kind of fucked up with the Finnish Snowboarding Association at the time we founded ours. So, we did not want to burn our reputation by going under that association: we wanted to do our own things.
>
> (p. 78)

With reference to Castells' concepts, this kind of agency among the women can be described as taking on a *resistance* identity – somewhat different to that of the Norwegian group, called the PowderPuff Girls, which I describe in Chapter 3 regarding snowboarding organisations. The PowderPuff Girls worked within the structure of the snowboard federation in Norway and the group can thus be described as having a *project* identity. This kind of identity produces social actors capable of building a new identity that redefines their position in society (or a given social institution), seeking to transform the overall social structure rather that either upholding or resisting dominant institutions. The Swedish participant (only one) held multiple organisational relationships with the Swedish Ski Association (of which snowboarding is included) as well as with commercial organisers. She worked as a teacher and coach and participated in women-only camps and sessions with the aim of promoting women's snowboarding and reducing gender differences in the sport. Her agency can also be defined as taking on a *project* identity. In terms of doing/undoing gender, it would seem reasonable to argue then that the agency of the participants from the Nordic countries reflect the undoing of

gender, as seen in their initiatives to bring about structural changes. Participants from Italy and Latvia, however, mainly associated with commercial organisers, and they revealed no effort to change the culture and organisation of
snowboarding, instead noting that they appreciated the kindness and thought-
fulness of the men in providing help and support. Based on the analysis, the
most suitable term to describe the agency of the Italian and Latvian athletes
was that of doing gender, meaning that they generally adhered to, and were
not actively trying to dismantle, conventional gender norms within the sport.

I will also briefly mention another of my studies (Sisjord, 2014), which
focused on adult snowboarders who attended a camp at a summer ski resort
in Norway. The intention of the study was to explore whether the participants had continued their 'youth activity' within a longstanding community,
or whether they began snowboarding as adults, so as to compare their various
experiences in participating in the snowboarding culture. I related the study
to Mannheim's elaboration of generational factors and Giddens' perspectives
of modernity and self-identity. A total of 11 men and 1 woman attended the
camp. The woman had anticipated the presence of other female snowboarders but became aware before the camp began that the other women who had
initially enrolled had since backed out. That did not stop her from attending,
however, as she said: 'It wasn't a problem for me, really, but someone else
might find it more difficult, handling the boy's locker-room humour, it's a bit
rough around the edges.' However, while she did say that she could handle the
situation perfectly well, she added: 'It's okay for a few days, but in the long
run I guess I might get the feeling of being around boys too much, in a way.'
It should be noted that the snowboarder in question was in her mid-thirties,
highly educated and seemingly a very independent person.

Gender at play in the contexts of secondary school and international top positions

This section is based on observations of the two secondary school coaches.
As noted above, a predominant belief was that male athletes are far more self-
driven, which also related to their daily lives outside of school. Both coaches
described male students as generally more passionate about snowboarding,
spending more time riding in their spare time – afternoons and weekends –
and in further educating themselves through videos and other visual channels.
Or simply, 'having a greater interest in it, or being more immersed' as the
male coach suggested. The female coach described this as such:

> The boys are more, like, snowboarders all the time. When they get home,
> they watch edits, or watch a film, maybe one they filmed themselves of
> each other, so they get home, edit it, maybe play a snowboarding game,
> and they generally talk a lot about snowboarding, they live it almost, it sort
> of becomes a lifestyle.

In contrast to the boys, her impression of the girls was that after school, the female students were more interested in doing other kinds of activities, such as spending time with their friends and having various leisure pursuits, commonly with people who are not involved in the snowboarding community. In addition, when they went for a training session they would commonly make off-snow training, for example, go for a run, instead of heading for the resort and terrain parks. She emphasised possible exceptions, however, this was her general view.

The fact that the male athletes appear more involved in the sport, as well as the snowboarding culture as a whole, seems to continue after having completed secondary school. The male students tend to keep the relationships they formed during this time, and they go snowboarding together, possibly travel abroad in the search for new opportunities, which is particularly true of those who aspire to a professional snowboarding carrier. The female students have fewer peers in their circles who also snowboard, which may result in their feeling lonely in the activity. Another element in their not pursuing snowboarding past secondary school was explained as their seeing friends who go on to continue their higher education, and thus many of them follow in the same direction, especially 'if they aren't particularly hooked on [the idea of] a professional career' as one of them expressed. The coaches felt that their observations and experiences from their time spent coaching secondary school students, that of male snowboarders supposedly being more driven and having more social reasons to continue snowboarding, may explain the lower number of elite female snowboarders.

Contrary to this, the WSF president, Satu Järvelä is a woman who has carved a space for herself in international, elite snowboarding. First, as a professional rider for several years, and then, when she stopped competing, as an international snowboarding judge. After that she became an agent for snowboarders, and she has been involved in arranging diverse kinds of events. She was also on the board of the Ticket to Ride (TTR) for many years. Thus, her history within the sport has proven that she is an enthusiastic, driven woman, both in her initiatives as the WSF president, and in her wider efforts in promoting women's snowboarding. Her narrative and personal experiences – in rising the ranks as a woman to hold a high position within the snowboarding industry – do also reveal challenges when it comes to recruiting more women into board positions, and generally in being accepted as a woman in male-dominated contexts. As she repeatedly expressed during the interview: 'I always have to prove myself, I have to be clear in my standpoints, and have the strength and will power to fight.' One of her stories worth including here, relates to her experience as an international snowboarding judge:

It's the same with the judging table, because there are most men, and few women. And with some, they want to see how far they can push you, like with the guy next to you, they want to see 'do you stick with your mind or opinion' or if your mind is easy to be changed. How many times I have fought with someone, you know guys like that: 'I saw this, this is how it goes.'

In this interview, Järvelä is passionate about rallying against the constant way in which men can patronise and put female snowboarders down, and that in her role, she wants to be a voice that can ensure that female snowboarders also stand their ground, and fight for their place in the sport.

The two examples of recent empirical findings, from the secondary school coaches and the WSF president, invite to reflections on changes in the overall snowboarding culture, and the recruitment of female participants on different levels. With reference to Thorpe (2005), a study which paints contrasting pictures of the female snowboarders and their participation in the sport, one more optimistic finding does indicate social progress, another of social constraint', and Laurendeau and Sharara (2008), suggesting the two scenarios of reproductive versus resistance agency, it seems reasonable not to be too optimistic in terms of more gender equality, although exceptions and more positive stories definitely exist. For example, women who have succeeded on the elite level in snowboarding, as will be presented in the following chapter.

References

Anderson, K. (1999). Snowboarding. The construction of gender in an emerging sport. *Journal of Sport and Social Issues, 23*(1), 55–79.

Laurendeau, J. & Sharara, N. (2008). 'Women could be every bit as good as guys'. Reproductive and resistant agency in two 'action' sports. *Journal of Sport and Social Issues, 32*(1), 24–47. DOI:10.1177/0193723507307819

Russell, K. & Lemon, J. (2012). 'Doing jibber': Female snowboarders negotiate their place in the snow. *Asia-Pacific Journal of Health, Sport and Physical Education, 3*(3), 239–252. DOI:1080/18377122.721741

Sisjord, M.K. (2009). Fast-girls, babes and the invisible girls. Gender relations in snowboarding. *Sport in Society, 12*(19), 1299–1316. DOI:1080/17430430903204801

Sisjord, M.K. (2012). Networking among women snowboarders: A study of participants at an international woman snowboard camp. *Scandinavian Journal of Medicine and Science in Sports, 22*(1), 73–84. DOI:10.1111/j.1600-0838

Sisjord, M.K. (2013). Women's snowboarding – Some experiences and perceptions of competitions. *Leisure Studies, 32*(5), 507–523. DOI:10.1111/j.1600-0838

Sisjord, M.K. (2014). When *grown-up kids* go snowboarding. A study of participants at a camp for adult snowboarders. *European Journal for Sport and Society, 11*(3), 205–226. DOI:10.1080/16138171.2014.11687942

Spowart, L. & Burrows, L. (2016). Negotiating moral terrain: Snowboarding mothers. In Thorpe, H. & Olive, R. (Eds.), *Women in Action Sport Cultures. Identity, Politics and Experience* (pp. 155–174). Palgrave Macmillan.

Spowart, L., Hughson, S. & Shaw, S. (2008). Snowboarding mums carve out fresh tracks: Resisting traditional motherhood discourse? *Annals of Leisure Research, 11*(1–2), 187–204. DOI:10.1080/11745398.2008.9686792

Thorpe, H. (2004). Embodied boarders: Snowboarding, status and style. *Waikato Journal of Education, 10*, 181–201.

Thorpe, H. (2005). Jibbing the gender order: Females in the snowboarding culture. *Sport in Society, 8*(1), 76–100. DOI:10.1080/1743043052000316632

Thorpe, H. (2009). Bourdieu, feminism and female physical culture: Gender reflexivity and the habitus-field complex. *Sociology of Sport Journal, 26*(4), 491–516.

Thorpe, H. (2011). *Snowboarding Bodies in Theory and Practice*. Palgrave Macmillan.

Thorpe, H. (2012). 'Sex, drug and snowboarding': (Il)legitimate definitions of taste and lifestyle in a physical youth culture. *Leisure Studies, 31*(1), 33–51. DOI:10.1080/02614367.2011.596556

7 Female elite snowboarders representing different epochs and snowboarding styles

This chapter introduces three former elite snowboarders – Åshild Lofthus, Stine Brun Kjeldaas and Kjersti Buaas – who represent snowboarding's different epochs and styles. The presentations are mainly based on qualitative interviews, with some of the information provided sourced from a master's thesis that examined the historical development of snowboarding in Norway from around 1985 to 1998 (Eltrheim, 2016). Much of the data in Eltrheim's thesis is based on newspaper articles and interviews conducted with some of the main figures within the snowboarding community at the time – the innovators as well as the high-ranking athletes.

The chosen snowboarders are not featured here with the intention of providing a biography or to focus on their athletic merits and accomplishments. Rather, they have been included in the sample as they all spent many years competing as highly ranked athletes internationally, and are thus ideal candidates to highlight the core themes of snowboarding's historical development.

This chapter focuses on how the athletes entered into the sport – their athletic backgrounds and how they got involved with snowboarding specifically. The focus will then move onto their careers through to when they stopped competing as professional snowboarders. The central elements of their careers which will be explored here are: their experiences as a member of a snowboarding team; training and practice; sponsors and prizes in snowboarding competitions. These will all be considered in light of the sport's relationship with gender.

Åshild Lofthus (born 1971)

Åshild Lofthus grew up in Southern Norway, in the small, rural village of Åmot in Vinje county, about three hours' drive west of Oslo, the capital of Norway. Her childhood featured a variety of sports activities: football, track and field, and skiing, the latter of which included cross-country/mountain, alpine and telemark skiing. When she first experimented with snowboarding, she would wear her telemark ski boots, and wore kind of old-fashioned clothing commonly used for telemark skiing, made of the specific wool fabric

DOI: 10.4324/9781003007098-7

called *frieze*. This specific clothing has long been worn for telemark skiing, which was first invented in about 1860 in Morgedal in Telemark, with Sondre Norheim considered to be the pioneer. He made his own skis and would head out on them in the wilderness, but he did also participate in the first skiing competitions too. The word *slalom* stems from this tradition (Bø, 1992), where the second part of the word – lom (originally *låm* in the local Norwegian dialect) – is best described as a slope or a track. The word *låm* was commonly combined with a prefix that referred to characteristics of the *låm*. The most demanding type, called *uvyrslåm*, refers to skiing in the wild and rugged nature, especially down steep hills (Kleppen, 1986), which may explain the reckless riding style. Indeed, only the most courageous skiers dared to try the uvyrslåm (Bø, 1992).

Åshild Lofthus is considered one of Norway's snowboarding pioneers (Eltrheim, 2016), the reason for which can be traced back to the milieu of which she grew up. For example, her brother, Einar Lofthus, was apparently the first to own a snowboard in their home village. He first tried to order one from the USA without succeeding, and instead then got the local shopkeeper, Harald Rishovd, to import one for him. Some years before, Rishovd had sold the Snurfer at his shop, so was obviously interested in this emerging new sport. He was active in the development of organised snowboarding as well, as the leader of the local snowboarding club and in founding the Norwegian Snowboard Federation (NSBF) in 1987.

The name of the snowboarding club – Uvyrslåmi Snobrettlag – is worth noting here. 'Uvyrslåmi' has been explained above, but the last word does specifically mean 'snowboarding club'. Another important factor about the name of this club is that Åmot, Åshild's home village, is geographically situated in the same area as Morgedal, thereby close to/part of the telemark skiing tradition. What is interesting about this is the association between this old style of skiing and snowboarding's 'anti-movement', rallying against traditional sport, originated on another continent. Could this be explained as an effect of globalisation – where new activities globally, may be locally adjusted and rooted in the existing culture and identity? Or, as suggested by Eltrheim (2016), was it a way to legitimise a new sport, perceived as something different, perhaps a bit frightening?

Uvyrslåmi Snobrettlag was one of the first snowboarding clubs in Norway. The club rapidly grew in numbers, with many skilled riders enticed to the club to participate. In addition to the Lofthus siblings, it's worth mentioning that Terje Haakonsen – known as 'the snowboarding legend' – entered the international snowboarding scene a couple of years after Åshild, then assumedly safe to have a clubmate and forerunner in the snowboarding community.

Åshild's entry into the sport is particularly noteworthy, especially given how quickly she developed her snowboarding skills. Together with a friend, her friend's brother, and her own brother Einar, she used to visit the local ski resort during weekends. The girls practised telemark skiing, but would occasionally be given the chance to try out their brothers' boards. Apparently, they recognised their sisters' skills and encouraged them to enrol in a Norway Cup competition, arranged by the club at the local ski resort. They did, and subsequently succeeded. After that, their interest in pursuing snowboarding gained momentum. Åshild travelled to other Norway Cup competitions with her club mates and continued winning. The year was 1987, she was a student at a secondary school that offered sport activities combined with the regular curriculum (similar with those mentioned in the discussions of school coaches who had been interviewed). The following year, she participated in a European Cup in Avoriaz in France alongside her brother and a few other club-mates. The story goes that the shopkeeper, Harald Rishovd, hired an old bus to drive the snowboarders to the contest. Because of that she was, literally and figuratively, on the road to success, as she explained 'I performed very well, so suddenly, several sponsors recognised me. Nobody had heard about me before.' Her achievements then led to a contract with Burton, who her brother was also signed with. The next step for the siblings was to attend the Burton camps in Austria the coming autumn, alongside riders from other countries. That winter she participated in a few World Cups, and in the summer, she was invited to a competition in Whistler, Canada, which ended up being a catalyst for her relationship with Burton, as she explained:

> And then, on the way home, one of the bosses of Burton drove me to the airport in Vancouver, and he presented me a contract which I signed, there at the airport. And I was like, yeah, probably all fine, so I just signed it. So yes, it was that simple.

That happened the summer before she was set to start her second year in school, although things didn't turn out that way, as she said: 'but, when I got the contract, I ended up doing that instead.' In the following years – five in total – she lived the professional snowboarding life, travelling around the world. When I referred to the page about her, on Wikipedia (in Norwegian), where she is described as Norway's 'most successful snowboarder' and asked for an overview of her merits, she answered:

> Yes, I guess I have, somewhere, but I …I finished in 93, that was my last year. I ended up with the World Championship in giant slalom and slalom, and World Cup combined, and European Championship in all disciplines, also combined. Yes, I had many combined victories [during those years], many World Cups and European Championships.

While discussing her snowboarding career we began with the Burton's Europe team. She felt very lucky to be included, given that Burton had one of the largest teams in the industry. The team consisted of six men, herself and a woman from Italy. The coach had previously coached the women on the

Austrian alpine team. A great deal of the autumn was spent on glaciers in the Alps, training on slopes from the morning, followed by endurance and strength training in the afternoon – very much like traditional alpine training. That was a change for Åshild, who used to practice during weekends in the winter season, and mainly just for fun. She easily got used to the situation, however, and felt very comfortable with her teammates as well as the coach. She never questioned the mixed-gender team, noting:

> Oh no, I never thought about it, I've always been the type of person to hang around with guys, always trained with the guys, so that was nothing, no, we had a very good relationship, just fantastic. Travelled around as a group all the time. We did everything together, so we were kind of like a family.

She further emphasised the benefits of training with male teammates as she would measure herself against them, rather than the women – the absolute best feeling was when she managed to beat them. Obviously, in her view she became a better snowboarder because of it.

With respect to gender issues in general, she repeatedly expressed never having experienced discrimination or not being respected as a woman, while also stating: 'But I think, I am not that kind of a person who would bother about such things, if you get what I mean.' She traces her standpoint further, to her life situation at that time she started her snowboarding career. For her, the professional snowboarding life was pure happiness, starting at the age of 16–17, being able to travel around the world, she said: 'it was just like a dream, doing what I liked most of all, I enjoyed every second.' She didn't care much about finances, she had all she needed, there was always someone caring for her and the team, organising the hotels, travels and such. When I more directly asked about money and sponsor contracts, she did clearly express that the male snowboarders, performing at the same level she was, earned much more than her. This was also acknowledged by her male teammates who commented on how bad her contract was, and encouraged her to renegotiate, which had apparently not occurred to her: 'I didn't really bother, spending time on that. I was just a simple girl from Vinje who could travel around the world, and that was worth more than all the money they could offer.' In a similar way, when I asked about prize money, she had not recognised, or could not remember, any differences between what the female and male riders received.

The 'dream' did however, end at a certain point. After five years, Åshild felt that she had experienced enough. She lost motivation, stating that, at a given point: 'you have seen all the same resorts and slopes, hotels, and, after five years, it wasn't exiting anymore, so the interest decreased.' She had accomplished what was possible, in a way. Although, another factor that affected her interest in the sport, was the changes that were occurring at the time, which she attributed to the FIS taking over more and more, so the sport became a lot more money-driven: 'It was so dumb, everything started to be controlled by money so it wasn't fun anymore, in any way.'

Åshild returned home, and took on a job as an instructor at the local ski resort – the place where it all started. She had intended to go back to school and prepare for further studies, possibly within physiotherapy, however, realised that this was no longer really an option, school was too far behind. She worked at the ski resort for a few years before going into healthcare, working in various positions within the community. Today, she is back working in the sports industry, at the local sports shop: 'It's all about coincidences, you know' – an expression she repeatedly uttered during the interview.

Stine Brun Kjeldaas (born 1975)

According to Eltrheim (2016), Stine Brun Kjeldaas was described an article in *Snowboardavisen* (The snowboarding paper) in 1993, as 'Norway's new shooting star'. This, stemming from the fact she had – as early as in her first season – won the Norwegian Championship and came fifth in the European Championship (Eltrheim, 2016, p. 61). You could also hypothesise that the phrase 'Norway's new shooting star' refers back to Åshild Lofthus, as a reference to Stine taking over from the recently retired professional snowboarder.

Stine's pathway into snowboarding shows some similarities to Åshild's. Stine grew up in Kongsberg, a town an hours' drive west of Oslo, with strong historical skiing roots. The town has a reputable ski resort, which gradually expanded the facilities it had to offer, and would go on to include one of the first half-pipes in the country, back in 1991 (Eltrheim, 2016). Stine lived close to the resort, so began downhill skiing at an early age, but without being involved with any kind of organised practice or competitions.

What she found most fascinating with skiing, was the off-piste forest trails that boarded the resort and the skiing on small jumps, where she regularly joined a group of boys. She would spend her time on the slopes like this, until she took an interest in snowboarding. She was given her male cousin's old board to ride on, which was way too big for her – far too long and heavy. Regardless – from then on, her main interest was snowboarding. It was a bit different, a new activity that was 'a little dangerous, and cool, and some kind of an underground culture, that I found very fascinating.' In addition to this fascination, she had noticed that the coolest guys were snowboarders and she was soon included in their group, one of whom became her boyfriend. After a while, her younger brother joined them, and they spent the evenings and weekends snowboarding in the half-pipe – it was all about having fun.

Gradually, Stine's interest in professional snowboarding was piqued, with her idols being Tina Basich, Shannon Dunn, and not least Nicole Angelrath from Switzerland. She followed her heroines on films and video, inspired by their accomplishments. She focused on skill enhancement and tried to do the same tricks as the group of guys she joined. When some of them suggested she should enrol in a competition she found that very strange, because she had never competed in sports, except for some synchronised swimming as a child – the only sport she had done outside of skiing and dancing. However, when the local ski resort should arrange a Norwegian Cup, she decided to give it a go. The year was 1993, and looking back at it now, she explained her reasoning for taking part: 'it was about two-three years after I had started [snowboarding], just for fun really, but since it was in Kongsberg and I was told "you have to try and sign up", I did.' When she ended up winning, it was to her own great surprise and joy. After that, she went on to participate in the remaining Norway Cup competitions that season and won them all.

As a result of her success in the Norwegian Cups she was selected to represent Norway at the European Championship in Avoriaz in France (1993), where she, as mentioned above made the fifth best ranking. While no national team existed at that time, the NSBF were responsible for arranging the Norwegian Cups and would select athletes from there to participate in other international championships. As she elaborated on the experiences from the European Championship she described it as unreal – to suddenly be that close to the stars she had long admired, and with the highest of the competition occurring when Nicole Angelrath approached her and complimented her on her riding.

When I noticed her quick progress, from unorganised 'snowboarding for fun' to competing in the Norway Cup and then almost directly to the European Cup – both of which she had in common with Åshild – she almost downplayed this trajectory: 'There weren't that many participating in the Norway Cup, probably about twelve', yet still admitting, however, that she did tend to score much higher than whoever came second and third, to which she explained:

> I think I'm quite competitive, so I kind of made up my own rules that I must get twenty points more than the next competitor, and gradually, I tried to push myself, because I wanted to be as good as Nicole, the World Champion, and I had decided on that quite early on, that I would be that good.

Stine continued snowboarding over the next two years, participating in the Norwegian Cups and the European Championship. She finished secondary school and reached the point that she had to consider her future plans. Maybe take a year off before going to university?

The plan to take just one year off from her studies, took another direction, due to her athletic success and the financial support that arose. Up to that point, she had just had low scale sponsors (e.g. for a board and boots), however, a change occurred when a sponsor called and offered to cover her travel expenses to World Cup competitions – first in Europe and if she succeeded there, then they might send her to Japan and the USA as well. The offer came from Duotone, a new brand from F 2 with a new collection. She accepted the invitation, as the only woman on the team with eight men, which included her younger brother for a short stint. She joined the team at the camps and training sessions, and soon participated in the first Continental Open – which was part of the World Cup – where she came second. After a few more competitions with positive results, she was sent 'to all master World Cups, to the USA and Japan, the whole deal'.

Then came the 1994–1995 season, and she attracted more sponsors. One being Prom, a company founded by Tina Basich and Shannon Dunn, and the first to produce snowboarding clothing for women – a bit different in style and colour compared to those designed for the male snowboarders. She would eventually go on to be sponsored by Quiksilver and Roxy and stayed with them for the rest of her professional career. These were great, financially stable companies, yet, she was still quite skeptical of them from the start, seeing as they were the companies that made boards for all types of board-sports, and didn't just specialise in snowboards.

After one year with Duotone, two more women were introduced to the team, something which she verbalised was a positive change. The main reason being that she felt more comfortable with female company even though she was used to her male teammates and wasn't too bothered about it. Another reason she noted, was the change she saw in her snowboarding practice; her new teammates did off-snow training which was new to her. Until then, she had just snowboarded and enjoyed the life with the team: 'it was like a very big group of friends travelling around the world, to Japan and USA, and Europe, and it was kind of, a lot of partying and fun, yes, it was really fun.' When her new teammates performed better than her, she realised that she needed to do more serious training, if she wanted to continue. At that time, the decision was being made to include snowboarding in the Olympic Games, which Stine found to be a very attractive prospect: 'that you could potentially be allowed to ride in the Olympics, that there might be a small chance, even though it seemed so far away.' She decided to continue and became part of the national snowboarding team, thereby enrolled in the body working under the Norwegian Olympic and Paralympic Committee and Confederation of Sport responsible for preparing the athletes for the Games. Through this, she experienced another type of a regular training regime, which seemed to work well.

Stine won a silver medal in the 1998 Olympic Games in Nagano. On her return home, she was met at the airport by a whole crowd of people, who took her directly to the main square in her home town. She was played music, drums and a song dedicated to her. According to Stine, it was very funny but also a bit too much, as she was not used to that kind of publicity. In retrospect, she elaborated on changes in snowboarding, after its inclusion in the IOC and with FIS now as the helm of the sport's official organising body:

It went from having this kind of rockstar image, to being seen more like traditional athletes, so the culture disappeared in a way, replaced by sports logos on everything and the outfit and what not, which all seemed wrong, compared to what the culture had originally been.

While she experienced some discomfort with the development of the sport, Stine did still continue her professional snowboarding career, with varying results. The season after Nagano was not a good one, as she reflected: 'After a while I got like, probably some kind of performance anxiety, I don't know, I got a bit shy and I felt a bit uncomfortable.' However, in the following seasons (2000–2003), she did very well, including in the World Cup and the X Games.

In terms of finances, she was doing well on that front too – during these years there was a lot of money in the sport. When it came to the prize money during the first few years of her career, however, men received more money than the women did for comparable rankings, which she felt was unjustifiable because 'I know I was doing as much as the guys, so in a way, it felt a bit unfair.' She revealed a bit of a different standpoint when asked about the sponsor contracts – she was certainly aware that the men were receiving better contracts and income, in comparison to the women riders of the same skill level and success. Yet, she didn't really speak out against it, since there were more men than women competing in the sport, and therefore more incentive for the sponsors to fund the male riders. The market value was apparently a good enough explanation, since the sponsors received more back from their investment in male snowboarders and their visibility.

A central factor in her ongoing success – despite the sport's prioritisation of her male counterparts – was its increasing focus on image and personality, not only the riders' athletic accomplishments. To have a spotlight in the niche media, doing films and videos, and meeting with the 'right' people at parties, doing the networking and so on, was apparently becoming a vital part of the popularity game. In that regard, she felt lucky in her way of performing and appearance, as she 'was one of the first girls who dared to be[have] like a girl, so I was very feminine compared to, many of the girls who thought they had to behave like boys, to be accepted.' This also refers to her riding style, as many women at that time believed that they had to adopt to the men's riding style to succeed, which also might impact on the judgement in competitions. She elaborated on her standpoint with a story from one of the Norwegian Cup competitions, when she entered the women's restroom, 'and the other girls [were] standing there, and were just like "what, do you wear makeup while snowboarding"' to which she answered, 'yes I do'. The general impression I got from Stine, was that she seemed aware of the fact that she was doing things her own way, and making her own style – in riding as well as in appearance.

After several years in professional snowboarding, and another unlucky performance in the 2002 Olympics, Stine decided to take up studies and enrolled at a programme for Culture and Communication at the University of Oslo, while still doing some snowboarding. Right before finishing her bachelor's degree, she was offered a job by Quiksilver and Roxy, which resulted in her spending eight years in Biarritz in France, starting out as Winter Marketing Manager and ending up as Head of Marketing for Roxy Europe. She also worked in various roles for the X Games. Today, she works for the International Døds (death diving) Federation (IDF) as Head of Sports and Media, in charge of the Døds Tour and the World Championship including all related broadcasts and TV series. Her affinity for death diving lies much in the culture, as she emphasises: 'it has some of the same spirit and community as snowboarding originally had'.

Kjersti Buaas (born 1982)

Kjersti Buaas was born in Trondheim, one of the largest cities in Norway, situated about a seven-hour's drive north of Oslo. Kjersti started snowboarding at the age of 12, inspired by her older sister, who she always strongly admired. She would first practice on small jumps she set up outside her family home. She found the sport more exciting and creative than skiing, which she had done as long as she could remember, as it was a favourable activity in her family – cross-country as well as downhill. Besides skiing, she played football, and attended dancing classes – jazz and classical – as her mother introduced Kjersti and her sisters to rhythmic activities from an early age.

In 1996, after two years of snowboarding, she participated in a big jump competition arranged by the local ski resort – Vassfjellet – which had its own Vassfjellet snowboarding club, of which her sister and all the 'cool guys' were members. She won the competition, recalling how she 'jumped high and far. I liked grabbing, but I wasn't really doing a trick or anything, more like a floaty air.' She wasn't particularly motivated by the competition per se, but she did enjoy the performance: 'I wasn't a typically competitive person, but I enjoyed performing. I liked the idea of showing off what I'd practiced'. Kjersti continued snowboarding at the same ski resort, where her mother used to be part of the skiing patrol. The resort had a small, not well maintained, and often icy half-pipe and sort of a big jump, where she had the opportunity to practice.

At the age of 15, after the 1996 Vassfjellet competition, she signed up for a national contest, at a ski resort in the Oslo region. The discipline was half-pipe and she performed very well in the senior class – the only class for women – which then eventually inspired her to pursue more competitions. Together with her friend, Lisa Wiik, from the same snowboarding club, she went to several Norway Cups with the two young women usually receiving first and second place. Kjersti's merits led her to join the national junior team, then consisting of just five young men. It didn't take long before she saw major success and went on to the World Junior Championship in 1999, which launched her international career. She was still in secondary school, but managed to combine schoolwork while travelling to participate in snowboarding contests around the world. In 2000, she signed her first professional snowboarding contract and won her first World Cup contest that same year.

This was just the start of her international snowboarding career, which would last for almost 20 years. She competed in the professional Snowboard Tour, World Cups and the X Games. She participated in four Olympic Games, the first was in 2002 in Salt Lake City, where she came fourth, the next in Turin in Italy, where she made the podium receiving the bronze medal. She is one of the few women who successfully has transitioned from half-pipe to slopestyle and big air, and in later years onto Freeride competitions.

After finishing secondary school, Kjersti had planned to pursue further education. Alongside being a professional snowboarder, she enrolled at university, eventually graduating with a bachelor's degree in Sports Science, which also included a minor in psychology. Her bachelor's thesis was actually referred in this book, in Chapter 4, focusing on injuries in snowboarding.

When I asked Kjersti about her experiences with mixed-gender teams she revealed a multi-faced relationship with the topic. During her time on the national junior team, she found it very exciting from the very beginning, a large part of that being because of the cool guys she was snowboarding with – all of whom snowboarded very well, and whom she admired. At the same time, she also found it challenging, because in that kind of environment, you had to act tough: 'first, [you had] to do what they did and fit in, in a way, and they talked about other things than girls of the same age, so that was difficult.' She added that to have counteracted this, it would have been better with one or more women on the team, as she explained:

Well, I think it was ok, on the slopes as well as off-snow. But of course, you compare yourself with those you train with, and the guys are usually more capable of jumping higher, lifting heavier, and doing more rotations. So, it does something to your self-confidence if it's always like that.

On the top of that, being the only woman on the team made her sometimes feel like an outsider in a male-dominated culture with a rather hard atmosphere. This was particularly obvious to her when they were travelling and hired a flat, for example, because they were all so close.

Consequently, she felt much better when she graduated to the senior team, where there were at least two other women. That was different, and very important for her, because 'it provide[d] a quite different energy and a different team spirit, then you have someone to identify with, and somehow more of a common ground.' She further expressed that it might have been better with a female coach too, while still emphasising that the male coaches had been very nice and tried to recognise everyone, and treat them equally. However, when it came to the more emotional matters, having female team-mates appeared even more important.

One of her new team-mates was Stine Brun Kjeldaas, who had been Kjersti's role model for quite a while – she was a huge fan. Stine was experienced and became a mentor for Kjersti, giving her advice about nutrition as well as how to prepare for competitions. Kjersti and Stine became very close as they were both now permanent members of the team until Stine stopped professional snowboarding in 2006. And even though Stine did usually perform better than Kjersti, that didn't hurt their friendship at all. In fact, they even have one particular funny story from a World Cup competition back in 2002 – they agreed to share the prize money if they both did well, which they did, coming first and second place, but this time with Kjersti taking first. That incidence and similar stories exemplified what she appreciated about snowboarding: having fun and supporting each other. Kjersti and Stine wanted to showcase snowboarding culture to people outside of the sport, so they established their own film production company – Brun-Buaas Production. They produced several films from different snowboarding contexts, included one following the national team on tour, so as to show viewers the sport's 'cool culture', friendship, and the snowboarding lifestyle. They even sent several films to a Norwegian TV company, which resulted in ten episodes in a programme series for teens. After Stine finished, Kjersti often felt lonely as a woman on the team, and therefore sought out connections with female snowboarders from other countries, which she found very satisfying, with many of these friendships forming through her sponsor team.

Kjersti was first sponsored by Burton. The contract covered her wages, which made it possible for her to continue working as a professional snowboarder. At a certain point, however, she found that she was no longer satisfied with the company, as she felt that even though they had a women's team it was still very male-focused. Eventually Kjersti found her way to Roxy which also had a separate team for women, in addition to female team managers, including Stine who worked for them after finishing her professional career. In her own words, Kjersti explains that the switch to Roxy was down to the fact that 'there was more room to be more feminine, and, yeah, you were more likely to have your ideas listened to.'

In terms of gender differences in sponsor contracts, she was clear on her standpoint that men are generally given much better contracts than women, except for the very few women at the top of the sport who probably earn about the same as the men, due to their heightened market value. She exemplified this statement with her own experiences, explaining that she had participated four times in the Olympics and won one medal, yet men performing on a lower level, who had probably never competed in the Olympics, were still earning far more than she ever did. Furthermore, she anticipated that possibilities for sponsor contracts had decreased in recent years, making it more difficult to make a living of snowboarding, more so for women than men because 'for the men, it's a bit easier to do films and have that sort of a lifestyle, for women I think it's difficult, as it always has been, but I think it's even more difficult now.'

In regard to the prize money, she revealed a similar opinion about the gender differences, but noted that changes had occurred during her time in the industry. In the early days, the quality of the prize might vary depending on the type of competition. For example, she recalled that before the World Snowboarding Tour was formally established and organised into an official tour, it was up to the individual organiser to decide on the prizes. What was particularly enlightening about this part of the interview was her current reflections on how the industry used to function which she hadn't really questioned back then. She used to believe that the men were performing more difficult tricks, and were therefore at higher risk for injury, but admitted that she had changed her mind on that: 'it's wrong to believe that, because there's also a risk for the women, probably even more, when looking at the slopes.' The reason behind her change of mind came from a 'wake up' in becoming more aware regarding gender issues and inequality in general, and personal experiences with suffering from injuries – a topic she elaborated on at the end of the interview.

When we eventually got to the question around why she chose to end her snowboarding career, she said that it was due to a 'mix of things' but mostly just because she had been doing it for so long – almost 20 years. She reached the point where she had achieved so much, and wanted to do something new, and take care of her body. Although she notes that she was not burdened with the fatal injuries, the sport had still taken a toll on her body, as exemplified with the several concussions she suffered and the injuries to ligaments in her knee and wrist. She also once damaged her teeth and lip during a photo-shoot when she was with a sponsor, which only goes to highlight what riders do in terms of extra duties for their sponsor. As a result, she decided to wrap up her career in a positive way, to make the decision herself, to focus on a healthier lifestyle.

During her final few years in professional snowboarding, she was inspired by her international friends and competitors to try out yoga and meditation, brain and breath training, and in eating healthier food. That led her to pursue training on yoga, meditation and breathwork for which she is now a certified instructor. She runs her own company called PRSNT (www.prsnt.co) offering courses and workshops that focus on a healthy lifestyle, physical activity, wellness, and nutritious food, often combined with outdoor life, for example skiing or snowboarding in the dramatic mountains peaks of Norway or in the deep, lightweight powder of Japan. Her customers come from a variety of backgrounds, mostly women, as PRSNT aims to create opportunities for women to come together and explore the breath, body, mind and nature. In response to my question about the end of her snowboarding career, she emphasised that although she had stopped competing, she hadn't actually stopped snowboarding altogether, as she explained:

> I still feel so connected and 'at home' when I'm out on the slopes, even now. When I strap my snowboard on and glide through the snow, I can easily find the feeling of being fully present. I believe it's a similar feeling

to what many are feeling when making art. Or singing. Or dancing. It's a dance on the snow where all things connect, my body, breath, mind and nature. All things that I love and what attracted me to snowboarding in the first place as a 12-year young Kjersti. Now that I am not competing it's like I can feel that feeling stronger, maybe because I'm back to the roots of it all. Playing and enjoying the movement. Just for the fun of it. What it all started with. I am a snowboarder at heart. Competitions can be powerful, but it's something so special, childlike, about not trying to perform. Just Being fully Present. I think that presence and purity can inspire people almost as much as someone winning a gold medal can.

References

Bø, O. (1992). *På ski gjennom historia* [*Skiing Through History*]. Det Norske Samlaget.
Eltrheim, A. (2016). *Norsk snøbretthistorie. En redegjørelse for norsk snøbretthistorie fra ca. 1985–1998* [*Norwegian Snowboarding History. An Account of Norwegian Snowboarding from c. 1985–1998*]. Universitetet i Sørøst-Norge. The University of South-Eastern Norway. The Faculty of Sport Science and Physical Education. Porsgrunn.
Kleppen, H. (1986). *På telemarkski. Ny stil i gamle spor* [*On Telemark Skis. New Style on Old Tracks*]. Det Norske Samlaget.

8 Concluding remarks

The presentation of the three elite snowboarders in the last chapter serves as a good reflection on the main themes discussed throughout the book. By representing different epochs as well as various snowboarding styles and disciplines, their narratives illustrate central aspects of the historical development of the sport. One vital aspect relates to the interviewees' affinity for the original snowboarding culture – some of its counterculture edge and the alternative lifestyle. Åshild and Stine were both critical of FIS's increasing involvement and organisation of the sport. Åshild revealed her opinion on this through a statement in her interview in which she said: 'everything started to be controlled by money, so it wasn't fun anymore, in a way'. In contrast to Åshild and Stine, Kjersti belongs to the generation where the situation is not really questioned: indeed today, the WSF and FIS seem to collaborate on shared responsibilities and duties surrounding elite snowboarding and mass/ recreational snowboarding, as discussed in Chapter 3. Yet, Kjersti's enthusiasm for the alternative lifestyle came through in several parts of the interview, for example, in her mentioning of the film production company she established alongside Stine – with its aim of presenting the snowboarding culture to younger people – and in her description of snowboarding as 'art', as exemplified in the last quotation.

Another interesting aspect of the three narratives, is how the women entered into competitive snowboarding. In contrast to 'traditional sports' – where participants are usually socialised into the sport through organised practice and competitions from early childhood – these athletes first enrolled in contests as teen-agers, and even then, it was basically just for fun. However, their immediate success in Norway Cups launched them into international competitions, which, from the outside seems like a rather quick trajectory into the sport's elite.

'It's all about coincidences, you know' Åshild Lofthus repeatedly uttered while she spoke about her snowboarding career, a phrase that certainly summarises her own understanding of her trajectory, with these 'coincidences' generally meaning that she was in the right place at the right time. However, it seems reasonable to dwell upon the statement. Arguably, her adolescence

DOI: 10.4324/9781003007098-8

almost set her up for success, in that she participated in several sporting activities, had an older brother who had been one of the innovators of snowboarding in Norway, and another particularly important factor, she was also part of a local snowboarding club led by someone who genuinely cared for the athletes and the sport. She used to spend her weekends at the local ski resort, where her interest in snowboarding grew. Likewise, Stine Brun Kjeldaas grew up in the neighbourhood of a ski resort, would mainly just ski with male friends, and was later included in a group of male snowboarders, who she wanted to match in terms of performance. Kjersti Buaas commonly visited the ski resort where her mother was part of a ski patrol, and her older sister and her friends used to practice there. These three examples then correspond to the heaps of research on socialisation and sport, where family and friends are perceived to be significant socialisation agents. In fact, this may also be explained in Bourdieu's terms with reference to various forms of capital – economic, cultural, social – and a sport/snowboarding habitus.

The three women mastered snowboarding and succeeded when they signed up for a competition. The next step then was for them to handle the various male-dominated contexts of the sport – on national and international teams – as well as 'all the extras' meaning sponsors, media and such. As an overall impression, they all seemed to find their place and managed the different situations well, although noting that more female company and possibly a female coach would have been preferable. They also recognised the unequal treatment of female and male riders in terms of funding – sponsor money and prizes (mostly in the early years of the sport) – yet, none of them really questioned these issues, and had seemingly accepted the practice and adjusted to the male standard, which seemed necessary if they were going to fit in in professional snowboarding. Two observations from Chapter 6 – concerning gender at play – may illustrate this point.

First, the stories from the coaches at the secondary school revealed different experiences in terms of gender differences. The male students were more into snowboarding 24/7 – training on their own, filming, studying their own performances – whereas their female counterparts mainly just snowboarded as part of the school curriculum, and less so in their own time. The coaches also indicated a narrower pathway for the female snowboarders after graduating from the school, when it came to moving on to higher levels in the sport. There were fewer female athletes, they had fewer opportunities for continuing skill development, and they tend to follow their female friends into further studies. The coaches' perceptions, however, are actually likely important reasons in themselves for the lower recruitment rate of female snowboarders in elite snowboarding.

Second, to enter professional snowboarding appears to be a question of 'survival of the fittest' which may be illustrated by Satu Järvelä's narrative. Satu comes across as a very independent and self-determined person. As a former elite snowboarder, international judge, and president of the WSF she definitely needed strength and courage to face challenging and unpleasant situations, to which her experiences as a judge is a pertinent example, specifically when other – male – judges tried to make her change her mind.

The male standard is even more obvious when it comes to contests where female and male snowboarders use the same facilities, without any differentiation with respect to gender. The practice seems to be well established and taken for granted among most of those involved. The interviewed elite snowboarders did not speak against it, but rather had seemingly accepted that you just had to adjust and make do. Similar perceptions came through in the media coverage of the World Championship held in Oslo, Norway in 2012 (see Chapter 4) where the size of the facilities was debated. The female participants who were interviewed spoke against any kind of gender differentiation; however, it is worth noting here that these very same voices were the ones who made the podium. This kind of debate occurs once in a while, as revealed by the coach of the recruit team when explaining the fact that it usually boils down to a question of finances. With respect to the recruitment of younger riders, it's worth reminding the reader of the female coach at the secondary school who admitted that she had changed her mind on that issue, because she felt that the female students weren't physically as capable of managing the facilities to the same degree as their male counterparts.

The issue around the facilities has also evoked scholars' interest in recent years. I have come across two studies that both focused on slopestyle. A vital focus of both studies was the risk of injuries versus optimal performance. One study conducted by Muñoz et al. (2018) focused on the effects of jump difficulty on the athletes' final performance in the slopestyle competition at the Olympic Games in Sochi, 2014, by analysing the three jumps versus the final score. Without going into the details, it is enough to mention the main findings: that men had better scores and more rotations in all jumps compared to the women. The authors conclude that the riders and their coaches have to 'weigh pros and cons of increasing the difficulty of jumps, or improve jumps that are already fluent in order to master them' (p. 20). Another study by colleagues at my own university – The Norwegian School of Sport Sciences – focused on participants in the World Cup slopestyle, for both skiers and snowboarders, has so far resulted in two master's theses. One thesis focused on how rider behaviour and equivalent fall height, and how these affect landing stability (Linløkken, 2022). Among the findings of this study were that there are greater differences between skiers and snowboarders than gender differences in general. The other thesis (Hoholm, 2022), studied 'pop' (referring to the action an athlete performs at the end of the kicker, at the point of take-off) and its relation to performance factors and the equivalent fall height among participants in the same contest. The main finding here was that both skiers and snowboarders – men and women – landed at the same distance and approached the point of take-off with similar velocities. Men had, however, longer flight time and higher vertical jump height compared to the women. The results are further discussed in relation to physical and biomechanical perspectives. As a closing comment on this emerging research within the natural sciences – specifically regarding facilities as well as the studies mentioned on physical requirements and injuries – it is reasonable to suggest that future research and expertise on the designing of snowboarding facilities should take into account the different groups of participants who are supposed to use them.

With reference to the latter, the crucial factors to keep in mind include gender, different age groups and levels of performance, as the facilities will have to cater to elite-level snowboarding, activities relating to the recruitment of younger snowboarders, and people of all ages who prefer just to snowboard on a recreational basis. This would require collaboration among several stakeholders – people in the industry as well as in snowboarding organisations. With respect to competitive snowboarding, which has been the main focus of this book, it is worth listening to the scholars who are providing knowledge and theoretical perspectives from sport governance in general. As Knoppers et al. (2019) remind us (as referred to in Chapter 3), it is important to look beyond gender proportional representation and organisational structures and identify other aspects such as discursive practices and the role that men and masculinity play in various contexts. This therefore means having a closer look at how people engage in practices of gender, and in so doing sustain or challenge inequality.

One piece of research from an adjacent topic to snowboarding, namely Wheaton and Thorpe's (2018) study on surfing and skateboarding, is relevant to include here. The focus of the study was the inclusion of the two sports in the Olympic Games, with the intention of exploring the potential opportunities and challenges for the female athletes and industry leaders as members of the international and national federations in the two sports. The results indicate that inclusion in the games would bring the sports 'from "afterthought" to center stage' (p. 334), which would mean greater visibility in terms of media attention and thus more sponsorships. Greater visibility may however, also have a negative effect considering for instance the sexualisation of the female body, as can be seen in surfing advertisements. The authors also discuss the immediate effect of visibility in relation to more serious structural issues, while not going as far as to challenge male-defined competition structures and rules. One idea going forward then might be to add event styles that suits women. Furthermore, the authors discuss the need for men to act as social agents, and how closer collaboration and support between men and women would be positive for achieving a more gender equal policy in the respective sport organisations. This, however, relies on men's awareness of their privileged position in a system permeated by hegemonic masculinity, and their willingness to change.

References

Hoholm, S.L. (2022). *"Pop" and Its Relation to Performance Factors and Equivalent Fall Height in World Cup Slopestyle for Skiers and Snowboarders.* Master thesis, Norwegian School of Sport Sciences, Department of Physical Performance.

Knoppers, A., Hovden, J. & Elling, A. (2019). Meta-analysis. Theoretical issues. In Elling, A., Hovden, J. & Knoppers, A. (Eds.), *Gender Diversity in European Sport Governance* (pp. 205–217). Routledge.

Linløkken, M.-S. (2022). *A Biomechanical Analysis of How Rider Behavior and Equivalent Fall Heigh Affect Landing Stability in World Cup Slopestyle for Freeski and Snowboard.* Master thesis, Norwegian School of Sport Sciences, Department of Physical Performance.

Muñoz, J., Garcia-Rubio, J., Ramos, D., León, K. & Collado-Mateo, D. (2018). Effects of jump difficulty on the final performance in snowboard-slopestyle-winter Olympic Games, Socchi, 2014. *Annuals of Applied Sport Science, 6*(2), 15–21. DOI:10.29252/aassjournal.6.2.15

Wheaton, B. & Thorpe, H. (2018). Action sports, the Olympic Games, and the opportunities and challenges for gender equity: The cases of surfing and skateboarding. *Journal of Sport and Social Issues, 42*(5), 315–342. DOI:10.1177/0193723518781230

Index

For Product Safety Concerns and Information please contact our EU
representative GPSR@taylorandfrancis.com
Taylor & Francis Verlag GmbH, Kaufingerstraße 24, 80331 München, Germany